# LEVERS OF
# ORGANIZATION
# DESIGN

# LEVERS OF ORGANIZATION DESIGN

*How Managers Use
Accountability Systems for
Greater Performance
and Commitment*

Robert Simons

HARVARD BUSINESS SCHOOL PRESS
BOSTON, MASSACHUSETTS

**Library of Congress Cataloging-in-Publication Data**

Simons, Robert.
    Levers of organization design: how managers use accountability
systems for greater performance and commitment / Robert Simons.
        p.   cm.
    Includes bibliographical references and index.
    ISBN 1-59139-283-7
    1. Organizational behavior.  2. Organizational change.
    3. Organization.  I. Title.
        HD58.7.S5824 2005
        658.4'02—dc22

                                                          2005004954

The paper used in this publication meets the minimum requirements of the
American National Standard for Information Sciences—Permanence of
Paper for Printed Library Materials, ANSI Z39.48-1992.

# CONTENTS

# PREFACE

IN THIS BOOK I argue that organization design is the most important determinant of success for implementing strategy in a large organization. I know that I have an uphill battle to prove my point. You are probably conjuring up images of managers mechanically shuffling boxes on an organization chart. You're also probably wondering whether this topic isn't of interest only to senior-level corporate executives or management consultants. You may ask, Wouldn't my time be better spent focusing on more important (and interesting) topics—strategy, technology, and leadership?

But if you want to understand how effective managers achieve outstanding results year after year, you must master organization design. All those who allocate resources to subordinates and hold them accountable for performance should know how to organize effectively—whether the organization they lead is a staff support group, a military tactical team, a business unit, or an entire company.

I won't deny that this topic is difficult. Until I started a new elective course at Harvard Business School two years ago, graduates from our MBA program received no training on how to design an organization. And Harvard is not alone. Very few business schools teach students how to design organizations effectively. Why? Because this topic transcends disciplinary lines:

to design an organization effectively, you need to understand business strategy, marketing, organization behavior, information technology, accounting, and leadership. The problem is that business schools are organized in ways that discourage interdisciplinary research and teaching. In other words, as with any other organization, the design of business schools influences our ability (or inability) to implement key objectives.

But if faculty instructors at business schools are not willing to deal with this interdisciplinary complexity, managers are given little choice. They must deal with organization design in its entirety and with all its messiness. It cannot be avoided.

Where can you turn for help? In recent years, writers have coined a dizzying array of buzzwords to help managers design organizations: networked organizations, transnational organizations, front-back organizations, boundaryless organizations, learning organizations, virtual organizations, federalist organizations, and individualized organizations, to name only a few.[1]

In reading these works, most readers, I'll bet, share my frustrations. With few exceptions, most writing on this topic either is utopian or offers practicums that have no theoretical underpinning. The utopians rail at the stifling nature of hierarchy and extol the virtues of organizations without structure: self-organizing work, networks, and employee empowerment will, they argue, drive out command-and-control empires. In practice—and with good reason—few managers are willing to abandon their organizations to this prescribed chaos.

The other set of books offers design choices supported by detailed lists of pros and cons. Yet these analyses quickly prove to be unsatisfying. Lists of tradeoffs and considerations fail to provide a clear sense of direction. When you finish a chapter, it is never clear exactly what managers should do—especially when the options spelled out in one chapter are affected by an equally confusing set of choices made in another chapter.

In this book, I present an integrated theory that gives clear direction about how to design organizations and align resources in specific circumstances. To do so, you will take a tour of strategy, marketing, accounting, organization theory, psychology, and information technology—applying best practice examples in a new way.

Chapters 1 and 2 set the stage by introducing the "levers" framework that anchors the book. Then in chapters 3 through 6 I introduce a series of "sliders"—like those found on a sound mixer. If you flip ahead through the book, you will see many diagrams of sliders that look like this:

These diagrams illustrate how to adjust the various design variables to achieve desired results. Sliders are developed for each of four "spans" that together will show you how to design an organization successfully.

Chapter 3 focuses on the definition of customer as the means of choosing the best structure for your organization and adjusting span of control, the first of the sliders. Chapter 4 describes how to use measurement and incentives systems to adjust the second slider, span of accountability. Chapter 5 discusses how to adjust span of influence to encourage people to interact with other units and encourage learning through the sharing of best practices. Chapter 6 introduces the final slider—span of support—to focus on the leadership principles that make an organization design come to life.

As you will learn, effective design is not a matter of adjusting each slider independently, but rather of understanding how they are set in relation to each other. For example, if you want an individual or business unit to be entrepreneurial, you can adjust the sliders to achieve this result.

The final two chapters illustrate how the model works by exploring the dynamics of organizing and aligning resources under different circumstances. You will learn how to balance the demand for organizational resources with the supply to ensure effective implementation of strategy. Chapter 7 analyzes three case studies that integrate the design principles from previous chapters. Chapter 8 provides action-based principles and illustrates how to apply the theory to achieve a dynamic equilibrium.

By the time you have completed this book, I am confident that you will understand why I believe that organization design is critically important for the successful implementation of strategy.

## ACKNOWLEDGMENTS

Now, some very important thank-yous are in order. This book is the outcome of more than five years of research encompassing field interviews, data collection, organizational analysis, and case writing. Ideas were tested in presentations to executive audiences, MBA students, and professional conferences. Along the way, many people were helpful in providing feedback and important suggestions for improving the ideas. In particular, I want to acknowledge the following individuals, who made suggestions for improvement of early drafts of this book: Joe Bower, Dennis Campbell, Jeff Cronin, Tony Dávila, Marc Epstein, Martin Evans, David Hawkins, Noorein Inamdar, Hilary Weston Joel, Bob Kaplan, Paul Lawrence, Mike Mahoney, Warren McFarlan, Kirsten Paust, David Rodriquez, Tatiana Sandino, Ben Shapiro, Pat Stocker, Michael Tushman, John Vogel, Harvard Business School seminar participants in Accounting & Control, Organization Behavior, and Marketing, and three anonymous reviewers.

Kirsten Paust played an important role in helping me design a new MBA course—Designing Organizations for Performance—that was instrumental in testing these ideas. The MBA students who enrolled in this course, some of whom are recognized in endnotes throughout the book, were more helpful than they can know in shaping these ideas. Before each class, I routinely handed out chapter drafts to serve as background reading for the analysis of specific case studies. After class, I would invariably return to my office with fresh ideas and insights that had arisen during our class discussions.

Special thanks go to my assistant Lisa Van Hazinga, who helped with manuscript preparation and provided feedback on all drafts, and to Kirsten Sandberg, my editor at Harvard Business School Press, who helped me along the way with important suggestions for improving the exposition and impact of the work. Sarah Weaver, production editor, and Betsy Hardinger, copy editor, applied their considerable skills to polish the final manuscript for publication.

Finally, I want to single out two people who acted as role models for important themes that underpin this book. Henry Mintzberg, my McGill teacher and longtime friend, taught me—through the constant creativity of his work—the importance of thinking out of the box. Tom Piper, a Harvard colleague and friend for the past twenty years, taught me—through his personal example—the importance of commitment to helping others.

To Henry and Tom, in particular, and to everyone else who offered assistance along the way, I thank you. Now, as Judy, my wife, has been reminding me lately, it's time to let go. I have enjoyed this project immensely. I hope that you find the ideas useful.

—Robert Simons
*Cohasset, Massachusetts*

# 1

## THE TENSIONS OF ORGANIZATION DESIGN

W E ARE BORN in hospitals, study in schools and universities, work in businesses and government, attend churches and synagogues, and belong to social clubs and volunteer groups. But do we have any sense of whether these organizations that affect our lives so deeply are properly designed? What tests should we apply to ensure that they are functioning as effectively as possible?

As we begin the twenty-first century, the forces affecting organizations have changed significantly from those of earlier generations. New technologies have increased productive capacity, markets have become global, the pace of competition has quickened, work has become more complex, and the capabilities of workers have been enhanced. Information technology, outsourcing, and alliances have changed the traditional boundaries of the firm.

Yet for all these changes, managers must still make the same critical decisions they did at the turn of the last century. Managers must still *design* the organizations they lead. Like any design activity, this is a creative exercise. Tensions must be balanced to create the desired effects. Managers must make choices about how to group individuals and structure their tasks. They must name units, choose leaders, and stipulate account-abilities. Although multiple alternatives may be considered, in the end only one organization design can prevail.

Decisions regarding organization design have profound and long-lasting effects. Consequently, some aspects of design are reserved for the highest levels of management. As John Browne, CEO of giant BP, states, "Senior leaders in any company do only a very few things. Ultimately, they have to make decisions on the organizational architecture and the way forward. They set poli-cies, standards, and targets, and create processes to ensure that people achieve or adhere to them."[1]

But the importance of organization design reaches far be-yond CEOs. Anyone who is responsible for achieving goals through other people must assign resources and decide how subordinates will work together. To be fully effective, all man-agers must understand the implications of design choices on the units they lead.

In the pages to follow, I offer a new theory of organization design that reflects the unique challenges now facing managers. This introductory chapter sets the stage by reviewing the ten-sions that managers must reconcile if they are to succeed in de-signing organizations for enduring performance. Chapter 2 presents an overview of the main model—what I call the levers framework—that anchors this book. My intent is to develop a set of design principles that provide sufficient knowledge to allow any manager to intervene and successfully change an or-ganization for enduring performance.[2]

## THE RISKS OF DOING NOTHING

Designing organizations, or fine-tuning them as circumstances change, is not an easy or straightforward task. The best designs must take into account a business's strategy, its life cycle, its competitive environment, and any number of other factors that may be relevant. So managers may be tempted to avoid altogether the task of designing their organizations. But research illustrates the potential consequences of doing nothing.

Businesses evolve over time, often following a predictable—and sometimes unhappy—path. In a punctuated equilibrium model first suggested by Greiner, periods of stability mask problems that ultimately erupt as a crisis.[3] As a consequence of doing nothing, existing management is often forced out of the business, to be replaced by others who can design an organization more in keeping with the changing needs of the business (figure 1-1).

Let's look at the stages. When an organization is first formed, business design typically receives little thought from the founding entrepreneurs. Everyone is a jack-of-all-trades. The fledgling organization is staffed with a small number of people who pitch in to help with sales, production, and record keeping. Enthusiasm abounds. New products, customers, and market opportunities allow creativity to percolate everywhere. The entrepreneurial firm is fun and invigorating. Adrenaline flows as everyone works together to put new products and services into the hands of customers. With luck, success leads to growth.

Over time, however, problems often emerge. Increasing size and complexity result in chaos and missed opportunities. The charisma of the founding entrepreneurs is no longer sufficient to manage a larger enterprise, leading to a *crisis of leadership*. At this juncture, the entrepreneurial founders are often forced out of the company.

As a result of this revolution, a new leader is hired to bring discipline and direction to the business. This new manager typically comes from a successful, mature business and brings the knowledge and experience to install systems and structures to get the business back on track.

**FIGURE 1-1**

## Stages of Organizational Growth and Crisis

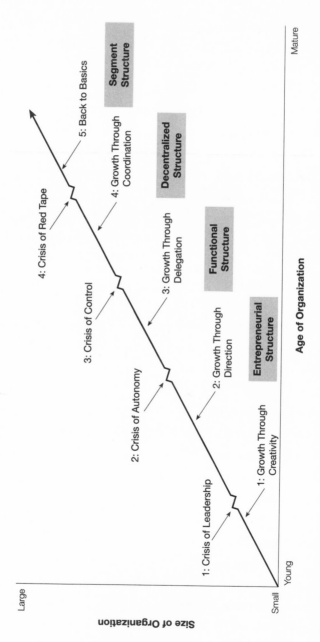

One of the new leader's first decisive actions is to set up separate business functions: sales and marketing, manufacturing, research and development, and accounting and finance. Individuals with specialized expertise and experience are hired to oversee these new functional departments. In contrast to the free-for-all that characterized the start-up phase, decision making becomes highly centralized. New rules and standard operating procedures are implemented and enforced. Discipline is imposed through the adoption of budgeting and inventory management techniques.

The firm resumes its growth. Unfortunately, specialization through functional orientation again brings unforeseen problems. Functional units become insulated from the marketplace, and the business begins to lose touch with its customers. Employees who joined during the exciting start-up years discover that the company is no longer a fun place to work. The discipline and centralized decision making have become stifling.

Frustration builds, leading to a *crisis of autonomy*. The leader is blamed for the loss of the entrepreneurial spirit that was the hallmark of the organization during its early years. Another revolution occurs. A new leader is recruited from a business known to delegate authority. Quickly, the new manager uses his or her experience to decentralize decision making. Stand-alone business units are created. Each product or regional group is given its own staff functions. Innovation is rekindled as the independent business units tailor their operations to respond to customer needs. Growth resumes.

As with the previous stages, however, growth through delegation creates its own set of problems. The decentralized structure creates independent fiefdoms whose unit managers are protected from the oversight of the head office. Coordination suffers, resources are wasted, and profitability declines—leading to a *crisis of control*.

Another revolution occurs. A new top management team is brought in to restore head office control and increase coordination between units. A segment structure is overlaid on the business units, and new centralized staff groups assume responsibility for planning, coordination, and resource allocation. Business unit managers must now obtain approval from powerful headquarters staff specialists before embarking on any major strategy commitment or allocation of resources. A great deal of time is devoted to meetings to set and review strategy, allocate resources, and evaluate segment performance.

Over time, as central staff groups become more powerful, yet another crisis occurs, this time a *crisis of red tape*. Operating managers feel that decision making has become burdensomely slow. A great deal of time is wasted in corporate staff meetings. More focused and nimble competitors are overtaking the company in the marketplace.

In the final stage, a new manager is again hired. This time, however, the mandate is to cut through the bureaucracy and get back to basics. The organization is radically simplified; noncore businesses are sold; centralized staff groups are dismantled; and direct accountability for results is again emphasized.[4]

A study by Miller and Friesen empirically substantiates the stages described by Greiner.[5] In line with Greiner's arguments that a lack of structural fit leads to crisis, Miller and Friesen identify four archetypes of unsuccessful firms:

- In the *impulsive firm*, organization designs are too primitive for the firm's rapid growth and increasing complexity. A small number of individuals dominate senior management. They make all the decisions but are too busy to deal effectively with mounting problems. This is equivalent to a firm on the verge of a crisis of leadership as illustrated in figure 1-1.

- The *stagnant bureaucracy* describes a highly bureaucratic organization in which top managers do not perceive the need to change structure or strategy. The firm suffers from centralized decision making and weak information systems. As a result, lower-tier managers feel ignored and alienated. As shown in figure 1-1, this is a firm suffering from a crisis of autonomy.

- The *headless giant* is characterized by fiefdoms of highly independent divisions. There is a lack of overall corporate leadership and coordination. Divisions operate independently without much regard for one another. This is a firm that figure 1-1 illustrates as facing a crisis of control.

- In the *aftermath organization*, a new management team attempts a turnaround by getting back to basics. But success is hampered because of scarce resources, the inexperience of new executives, and inadequate administrative infrastructures. This is the back-to-basics stage shown in figure 1-1.

The risks of doing nothing are substantial. If managers don't adjust the design of their organization with changing circumstances, underperformance is inevitable. Sometimes, existing management may have to be replaced by others who can and will make tough choices and substantive design changes.

## THE FOUR TENSIONS OF ORGANIZATION DESIGN

To anticipate and avoid the crises just described, managers must design organizations that can adapt over time. Accordingly, as you study the ideas and design principles of this book, you must be sensitive to the need to reconcile the tensions between:

- Strategy and structure

- Accountability and adaptability

• Ladders and rings

• Self-interest and mission success

These tensions are illustrated in figure 1-2, a diagram that you'll revisit in different forms throughout this book.

## The Tension Between Strategy and Structure

The picture that emerges from the life cycle analysis is a deterministic view of organization design. Size and time—the two axes of figure 1-1—are the driving forces of both organization design and organizational crisis. But the markets in which organizations compete are also constantly changing. Over the past several decades, markets have become much more customer focused. With advancing technology and decreasing prices, product life cycles have been shrinking rapidly. New information

**FIGURE 1-2**

**Tensions of Organization Design**

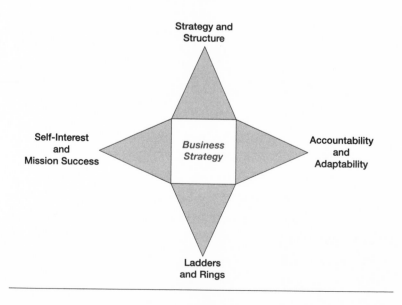

technologies have increased both the speed and the intensity of competition.

Organization designs must evolve to reflect these changes. As markets have become more customer focused, successful companies—from General Motors to IBM—have transformed themselves from the rigid bureaucracies of past eras to become much more responsive to their markets.

It seems clear that an organization's design should reflect its business strategy: analyze the situation, decide what to do, and then organize to do it. But managers must configure resources not only to get work done but also to learn and respond to changing circumstances. As a result, managers must design their organization to implement today's strategy and also to foster the flow of new ideas that will stimulate the formation of tomorrow's strategies.

Thus, it's a two-way street. On the one hand, structure follows strategy. But on the other hand, organization design—through its defining effect on information flows—influences future strategies. The structure of an organization determines how information from the market is processed and acted upon. The design of an organization determines who receives information, to whom it is forwarded, and what actions are ultimately taken. In other words, not only does strategy determine structure, but structure also determines strategy. This two-way flow must be incorporated into any successful design.

## The Tension Between Accountability and Adaptability

In past eras, accountability for results was reserved for top-level managers, who assigned specific tasks to workers and ensured compliance with standard operating procedures. Now, rather than specify *how* subordinates should do their jobs and monitor compliance, managers at all levels place much more emphasis on *accountability for results*—leaving the actual decisions about how to achieve these results to the initiative of the workers involved. Quality circles, self-organizing production teams, and performance evaluation systems based on customer satisfaction all reflect increased accountability for outcomes at all levels in the organization.

This increase in accountability is also evident in government and public service agencies. Instead of compliance with preset standards of operations, appointed officials are increasingly being held accountable for measurable outputs and results. School superintendents are no longer asked only to deliver the required educational curriculum; they are also accountable for student test scores and graduation rates. For police commissioners, ensuring that patrols are on schedule is no longer sufficient; they are accountable for public safety and crime rates.

A tension arises, however, because organizations must also, in addition to achieving results, retain their ability to experiment and adapt. Employees must be encouraged to test new ideas. Businesses must continually devote scarce resources to innovation.

So a tension inevitably exists between accountability for today's goals and adaptability for the future: on the one hand, managers must achieve short-term results; on the other hand, they must also ensure that the organization retains the ability to innovate and adapt. Both objectives must be incorporated into effective designs.

## The Tension Between Ladders and Rings

Organization charts typically show senior managers sitting at the apex of a cascading pyramid of power and authority. Each rung below them represents a subordinate position in the ladder of accountability. These cascading hierarchies are designed to efficiently move information up and down. Thus, they are sometimes pejoratively referred to as silos, chimneys, or stovepipes.

More often than not, however, workflows must be coordinated not only up and down but also across the hierarchy. To coordinate complex workflows, information and resources must be shared across units. The nub of the problem, of course, is the difficulty of coordinating activities when employees do not control all the information and resources they need to get the job done. People must find ways to influence individuals in other units who are not accountable to them. As a result, successful organization designs must take into account not only the vertical hierarchy—the ladders—but also the horizontal networks—the rings—needed to coordinate information, decisions, and workflows.

Technology has greatly enhanced the ability of managers to create such horizontal networks. Information can now be captured, analyzed, and shared in unprecedented ways. Intranets and employee portals allow companies to easily disseminate information to employees, and for employees to pull information from new tools and databases to help them organize their work. New measurement techniques allow managers to evaluate the contribution of cross-unit activities. To fully leverage these capabilities, new and emerging techniques must be part of our designs.

## The Tension Between Self-Interest and Mission Success

Because organizations are groups of people, no theory of organization can be complete unless it addresses head-on its embedded assumptions about human behavior. Can we assume that people will use their information and power to advance the organization's best interests? Or will they choose to maximize their own well-being?

The view of human nature in organizations has changed dramatically over the past century. A hundred years ago, employees were seen as something close to indentured, performing heavy or repetitive labor for a subsistence wage. By the 1950s, following the industrialization that supported two world wars, newly trained workers achieved an unprecedented level of middle-class affluence. But the dark side of increased material wealth was the forced conformity described in Sloan Wilson's celebrated period novel, *The Man in the Gray Flannel Suit*. Employees were expected to subordinate their personalities and acquiesce unquestioningly to the demands of the corporation and its top management.

In the 1980s and 1990s, the tide began to turn. As markets became increasingly customer focused, managers realized that they could no longer issue orders. Instead, decision making was delegated to front-line employees, who were empowered to respond to the information they were receiving from customers. Employees had now become critical partners in implementing strategy.

From indentured laborers, to corporate conformity, to empowered partners. What assumptions about human nature are appropriate in a theory of organization design for the twenty-first century? In a book titled *Designing Organizations to Create Value*, Brickley et al. describe three models of human behavior that underlie previous theories of organizations. They label the first model "Only-Money-Matters." In this view, financial incentives are the sole motivator of human activity. The second model, "Happy-Is-Productive," is predicated on the belief that employee satisfaction will result in high productivity. The final model, "Good-Citizen," argues that people are intrinsically motivated and take pride in their work, and therefore they naturally want to excel.[6]

Recognizing that each model contains a little truth, the authors offer the standard economic assumptions about human behavior:

We base our analysis on two fundamental concepts: People tend to act in their own perceived self-interest, and people's knowledge bases differ. Successful organizations assign decision authority in a way that effectively links that authority with the relevant knowledge . . . [through] performance measurement systems and compensation programs that provide self-interested decision makers with the incentive to use their knowledge to make decisions that increase shareholder value.[7]

Economists believe that individuals are invariably driven by self-interest. But this choice may not be predetermined. In some circumstances (e.g., a military tactical unit), individuals may choose to sacrifice self-interest in pursuit of mission-based goals. The U.S. Marine Corps, for example, proudly honors the legacy of Private First Class James Anderson Jr., who wrapped his body around an exploding enemy grenade to protect the lives of those around him.[8]

In this book, I recognize that every individual in every organization makes a series of critically important decisions: Should I work toward (1) my own self-interest, (2) the goals of the subunit to which I belong, or (3) the goals of the overall organization taken as a whole? These decisions—made independently by countless individuals throughout any business—affect how resources are allocated, how information is shared, and how likely it is that the organization will achieve its goals.

Managers must therefore recognize in their organization designs the inevitable tension between self-interest and mission-based goals. I devote an entire chapter (chapter 6) to a consideration of how human behavior is in itself a design variable, and how managers can alter individual behavior to fit the designs of the organizations they lead.

# THE ORGANIZATION OF THE
# REMAINING CHAPTERS

In laying out this new theory, I will follow the same path as an architect designing a building: designing the physical space and layout (chapter 3), installing the various electrical and temperature control systems (chapter 4), ensuring that the building supports the multifaceted needs of the occupants (chapter 5), and, finally, ensuring that the building attracts the right occupants (chapter 6). Then we will look at several organizations to explain how to integrate these principles (chapter 7).

Unlike the architect who works with steel and concrete, however, I recognize that the job of designing a living organization is never finished: any organization operating in competitive and dynamic markets must be both flexible and adaptive. Accordingly, I end the book (chapter 8) by developing a dynamic framework that will allow managers as well as scholars to understand the principles of changing organization designs over time.

To guide you in the detailed analyses that follow, chapter 2 presents an overview of the framework, which is based on the concept of levers of organization design.

### CHAPTER THEME

Effective organization design requires balancing a series of tensions.

### KEY CHAPTER IDEAS

- Understanding the principles of organization design is important for managers at all levels.

- Managers can avoid crises and failures by adopting principles of organization design that lead to a dynamic, ongoing alignment of resources.

- Balancing four sets of tensions is the key to successful organization design:
  - Strategy and structure
  - Accountability and adaptability
  - Ladders and rings
  - Self-interest and mission success

## ACTION STEPS

Rank order, or otherwise decide which of the following tensions are most important in the design of your organization.

| | | |
|---|---|---|
| • Strategy | ←→ | Structure |
| • Accountability | ←→ | Adaptability |
| • Ladders | ←→ | Rings |
| • Self-Interest | ←→ | Mission Success |

# 2

---

# ALIGNING SPAN OF

# ATTENTION

THIS CHAPTER PRESENTS an overview of the levers of organization design framework and previews the chapters ahead. The focus—consistent with the rest of the book—is on developing design principles for organizations where customers are demanding, competition is intense, products and services are complex, and people are widely dispersed.

At the outset of the journey, you should be clear on the perspective that we are adopting. For our purposes, *organization design* refers to the formal system of accountability that defines key positions in an organization and legitimates rights to set goals, receive information, and influence the work of others.

Several aspects of this definition are important. First, *accountability*—the major organizing concept of this book—is at the heart of organization design. The simple sign "The Buck

Stops Here"—made famous by its place of prominence on President Harry Truman's desk—signals ultimate accountability for decision making. When people are accountable, they are answerable for performance on some measured dimension: units of output, dollars of profit, or national security.

This implies that organization design is not a democratic activity. But, as I shall discuss at length, even though some aspects of design may be reserved for senior managers, employees at all levels need to understand how the levers of design can be manipulated to maximize the efficiency and effectiveness of their own units and groups. Starting with the separation of owners and senior executives and ending with the specific goals that each employee is expected to achieve, any business organization is a cascading hierarchy of accountability. Each employee or manager is accountable to superiors higher in the hierarchy.

Second, our focus will be primarily on *positions*. Over time, individuals come and go, but the system of accountability rests with the position itself. It is these positions—and the rights that go with them—that provide the road map of roles for every individual in the organization.

The final part of the definition reminds us that organization design is the principal mechanism for legitimating authority and power through *formal rights*. In a cascading process, each manager in the organization stipulates the rights of subordinates to (1) receive information, (2) set specific goals for subordinates, and (3) influence the decisions of others. With rights, of course, come responsibilities. The right to receive information confers the responsibility to send information to superiors; the right to set goals brings the responsibility to ensure that those goals reflect the needs of the organization; and the right to influence the decisions of others carries with it the responsibility to assist others in support of organizational purpose.

# THE FOUR CS OF ORGANIZATION DESIGN

The framework for the theory to be developed in this book is illustrated in figure 2-1. We start with strategy at the center of the diagram and then analyze four determinants—the "four Cs"—that will yield the solution to designing organizations that ensure the successful execution of unique strategies.

The four Cs that must be analyzed *before* any successful organization design are as follows:

- Customer definition

- Critical performance variables

- Creative tension

- Commitment to others

**FIGURE 2-1**

**Levers of Organization Design**

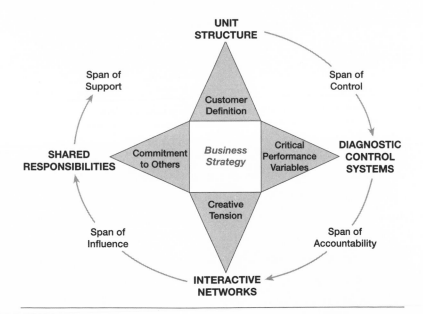

**Customer Definition**

We start our analysis by identifying the organization's primary customer. In an era when there is a tendency to call everyone a customer, this analysis is sometimes difficult, but it is essential. As illustrated by the compass orientation of figure 2-1, this is the "true north" of organization design.

Defining a primary customer focuses on strategy as position: gaining an understanding of the organization's market position relative to the needs of its customers and the positioning of competitors.[1] Michael Porter's "five forces" analysis is the best-known application of strategic positioning analysis.[2] In this framework, five forces—customers, suppliers, substitute products, the threat of new industry entrants, and interfirm rivalry—determine both the profitability of an industry and the market positions that are most likely to achieve competitive advantage.

Analysis of the primary customer provides the insight needed to design lever 1: *unit structure*. This lever will begin to reconcile the tension between structure and strategy identified in chapter 1. Alternative designs will be explored to ensure that structure responds efficiently and effectively to customer needs.

**Critical Performance Variables**

With unit groupings in place, the next step is to determine the *critical performance variables* that underpin the successful implementation of strategy.

This part of the analysis focuses on strategy as plans: understanding strategic intentions, tactics, and milestones. You can imagine a military commander using maps, intelligence, and assessment of relative force strength to work out battle plans.

These plans are communicated to field commanders, who are given responsibility for executing the orders using the resources under their control.

In a business, this function is often described as strategic planning: the formal tools and systems used to formulate objectives, analyze strategic options, and communicate action plans to ensure the achievement of important organization goals.

Analysis of critical performance variables gives managers the information they need to design lever 2: *diagnostic control systems*. You will learn how top managers create these systems to support business plans and the overall strategy of the business. You will explore in detail the power and design of financial accountability systems (e.g., profit plans), nonfinancial accountability systems (e.g., balanced scorecards), and incentive systems. This analysis will show you how managers can balance the second tension discussed in chapter 1—the tension between accountability and adaptability.

## Creative Tension

Unit groupings and accountability systems are not the end of the story. The previous two definitions of strategy—as position and plans—emphasize formal analysis based on market position and strategic goals. However, managers must also consider the extent to which their designs foster the development of new ideas that can become tomorrow's strategy. This is strategy as emerging patterns of action.

Using a variety of mechanisms to stimulate the creation and sharing of new ideas, organizations must support the capacity to learn. Organization designs must encourage individuals to interact and communicate horizontally with those in other units. This is the tension of ladders and rings referred to in chapter 1. In addition to top-down planning, managers must also design lever 3: *interactive networks*. These networks promote bottom-up and lateral information flows.

To understand how to design interactive networks, we must analyze the level of *creative tension* that is needed to support a business's strategy. For some strategies to be successful, managers must encourage people to experiment, overcome obstacles, and share new information. Faced with challenges, people often invent creative solutions. Such was the case when engineers at Analog Devices discovered that a silicon chip they were testing vibrated unacceptably under impact. Engineers began looking for applications where this property could be used to advantage, leading to the chip, now found in every automobile, that fires airbags during rapid deceleration.[3] Similar stories of product creativity have been told for 3M's Post-it notes—a product created to find a use for a weak adhesive derived accidentally in the lab—and for Procter & Gamble's floating Ivory soap, a result of excess air in the product when an employee forgot to turn off the soap machine during a lunch break. Sometimes, the duplication of successful initiatives may lead to entirely new strategies, such as Analog Devices' new micromachine business based on the vibrating chip.

## Commitment to Others

Unit structure, diagnostic control systems, and interactive networks cannot function properly unless senior managers are able to influence the willingness of people throughout the business to pitch in and support others. This is strategy as perspective, reflecting an organization's history, culture, and top management style.

An important part of strategy is to shape how individuals behave in their day-to-day work. In some circumstances, strong commitment to others will be essential for the successful implementation of strategy; in other cases, commitment to helping others will be less important for success.

When commitment to others needs to be strong, managers must design lever 4: *shared responsibilities*. This involves specifying not only rights (to set goals, receive information, and influence the work of others) but also responsibilities—and then holding subordinates accountable for those responsibilities.

## ALIGNING SPAN OF ATTENTION

Although the discussion here will necessarily be about formal positions, structures, and measurement systems, we will move quickly to the impact of these choices on individual people. Above all else, our goal is to understand how to create structures and accountability systems that influence how people do their work and where they focus their attention.

Accordingly, I should emphasize now that the levers of organization design are merely a means to an end. They are the means by which managers influence *span of attention*, which I define as the domain of activities that are within a manager's field of view.[4] Span of attention describes what people pay attention to, collect data on, and react to through their actions. As you will see, aligning the span of attention for each person and unit throughout the organization will be the key to ensuring the successful implementation of strategy.

The concept of spans is a central tool in our design toolkit. A dictionary defines *span* as the spread between two limits. For example, a bridge could be described as having a wide or narrow span; Japan's 2.4-mile Akashi-Kaikyo Bridge is reported to have the widest span of any bridge in the world.

In a similar way, span of attention can be either narrow or wide. A person has a narrow span of attention if he operates in a carefully defined and constrained sphere of activities—for example, performing routinized activities on an assembly line. His range of peripheral vision is very small. By contrast, an individual has a wide span of attention if he gathers data, interacts, and attempts to influence wide swaths of an organization. For example, a manager of a business unit may pay attention not only to customer markets and the activities of his unit, but also to the activities of other internal units that source materials and provide shared services. To be effective in this case, the manager's peripheral vision—his span of attention—must be very wide.

The span of a bridge is supported by a variety of suspension cables, arches, trusses, and girders. Similarly, managers have a variety of devices at their disposal to shape and support span of attention. Here, we will focus on four organizational spans that collectively determine span of attention. Together, these four spans define what an individual pays attention to. Two of the spans are "hard" spans—created through formal rights and responsibilities—and two are "soft" spans—created through informal networks and patterns of behavior.

Managers can (and should) adjust each of these four spans to be either narrow or wide. These spans provide answers to the critical questions posed by employees in every organization:

- *Span of control:* "What resources do I control to get my job done?"

Few          Many
Resources    Resources

  Span of control defines the range of resources for which individuals are given decision rights and are held accountable for performance. Unit structure (lever 1) is the means by which managers place resources in the hands of the individuals who occupy various positions in the organization.

- *Span of accountability:* "What measures will be used to evaluate my performance?"

Measures Allow Few Tradeoffs — Measures Allow Many Tradeoffs

In designing diagnostic control systems (lever 2), we will focus extensively on span of accountability, defined as the range of tradeoffs embedded in performance measures used to evaluate a manager's achievement. As you will see, the relationship between span of control and span of accountability has important implications for innovation and entrepreneurship.

- *Span of influence:* "Who do I need to interact with and influence to achieve the goals for which I'm accountable?"

Interactions Within Unit — Interactions Across Units

Span of influence defines how wide a net an individual casts in collecting data, probing for new information, and attempting to influence the work of others. Span of influence can be adjusted using lever 3—interactive networks. As with the other spans, managers may want the span of influence to be wide in some circumstances; in other cases, the span of influence will be set more narrowly.

- *Span of support:* "How much support can I expect when I reach out to others for help?"

No Commitment to Help Others — Strong Commitment to Help Others

Span of support defines the range of support that an individual can anticipate and expect from people affiliated with other organizational units. Depending on the strategy of the business and the levels of the other spans, managers may wish to set this span wide or narrow. Using lever 4—shared responsibilities—we will discuss the ramifications of this choice and the conditions that are necessary to build a wide span of support.

**Aligning the Spans**

To align span of attention and ensure the successful implementation of strategy, I will show that the supply and demand for organizational resources must be in balance for every individual and unit. To achieve this alignment, managers must achieve the following equality:

$$\text{Supply of Resources} \quad = \quad \text{Demand for Resources}$$

$$\text{or}$$

$$\frac{\text{Span of}}{\text{Control}} + \frac{\text{Span of}}{\text{Support}} = \frac{\text{Span of}}{\text{Accountability}} + \frac{\text{Span of}}{\text{Influence}}$$

In chapter 8, I provide a test that can be used to determine whether this equilibrium exists for an individual position, a business unit, or an entire business. To illustrate how to adjust the spans to achieve or fine-tune this alignment, I will show you how to analyze the four Cs and their respective design levers: unit structure, diagnostic control systems, interactive networks, and shared responsibilities. Again, however, I remind you that this detailed work is merely the means to an end: our ultimate goal is to align the span of attention for all individuals in the organization so that their work will be focused appropriately on the implementation of strategy.

## Past Themes of Organization Design

Before we embark on a detailed analysis of the levers framework, it is helpful to remember important work that has preceded us. Modern organization theory originated with German sociologist Max Weber (1864–1920), who coined the term *bureaucracy* to describe the ideal organization type: one that promotes efficiency through specialization, hierarchy of authority, predictable rules, a focus on positions rather than personalities, and rewards based on merit.[5] A variety of scholars have since offered theories and prescriptions to describe how best to design modern organizations. Five of these ideas, in particular, form an important foundation for the theory to be developed in this book.

**Strategy Shapes Structure.** The first idea, developed by business historian Alfred Chandler, recognizes that organization design is a response to the specific aims of the organization.[6] Studying the evolution of large companies such as DuPont, General Motors, and Sears, Chandler was the first to recognize that organization design must be molded to facilitate the accomplishment of organizational goals, such as growth or expansion into new markets. I will follow Chandler's lead and argue that both market competition and management's strategy are key variables in the design of any business organization.

**People Have Limited Attention.** Nobel laureate Herbert Simon identified human attention as a critical variable in the design and functioning of organizations.[7] Simon argued that individuals are limited in their capacity to process information and are therefore forced to make choices about where to allocate their scarce attention. This insight is important for the design of organizations because it acknowledges that formal structures and routines influence the information that people consider and the actions they undertake. As you will see, the concept of scarce management attention will be an important and recurring theme of this book.

**Organizations Process Information.** The third idea, articulated by Jay Galbraith, conceptualizes the entire organization as an information processing entity.[8] In this view, organizations are designed primarily to process information to deal with various levels of uncertainty. Galbraith proposed that higher levels of uncertainty require greater capacity to process information, either by reducing uncertainty or by using mechanisms such as formal hierarchies and lateral information linkages to process information more efficiently. In the theories developed in this book, managing information flows will also be a central theme.

**Units Must Be Differentiated and Integrated.** The fourth concept, developed by Paul Lawrence and Jay Lorsch, recognizes the need to create organizations that are both differentiated (to allow specialization and economies of scale) and integrated (to coordinate workflows and interdependent goals).[9] For example, sales offices and production plants are typically managed separately (i.e., differentiated) because they focus on different types of issues and goals: the sales office focuses on markets, customers, and competitors; the production plant focuses on equipment, raw materials, and labor markets. However, mechanisms must integrate the activities of these independent units to coordinate workflows. In the chapters to follow, you will learn how to achieve scale economies and market responsiveness by separating and integrating organizational units.

**Designs Are Built on Archetypes.** The final idea, pioneered by Henry Mintzberg and Danny Miller, introduces organizational archetypes as tools of design.[10] Rather than thinking about endless permutations and combinations of design variables, these authors argued that there are in fact only a small number of configurations that describe most organization forms. We can develop these archetypes by studying the choices that managers make in different circumstances. Following Mintzberg and Miller, I identify—starting in chapter 3—the attributes of a small number of archetypes that can serve as models for modern organization design.

Aligning span of attention for each person and unit in an organization is the key objective of organization design.

- *Definition:* Organization design refers to the formal system of accountability that defines key positions in an organization and legitimates rights to set goals, receive information, and influence the work of others.

- *Definition:* Span of attention is the domain of activities that are within a manager's field of view.

- As a prerequisite to applying the levers of organization design, four variables (the four Cs) must be analyzed and understood:

| **Analyze** → | **Levers** |
|---|---|
| Customer Definition | Unit Structure |
| Critical Performance Variables | Diagnostic Control Systems |
| Creative Tension | Interactive Networks |
| Commitment to Others | Shared Responsibilities |

- The levers of organization design are a means to an end. They are used to adjust four interrelated spans that collectively shape span of attention:
  - Span of control
  - Span of accountability
  - Span of influence
  - Span of support

## ACTION STEPS

In preparation for designing an organization, clarify and
agree on the four Ps of strategy:

- *Position:* Who are your organization's major
  competitors? What are their relative strengths and
  weaknesses? How are your products and services
  differentiated from those of competitors?

- *Plans:* What are the major plans and initiatives of
  your organization? How is success measured?

- *Patterns of action:* To what extent are innovation and responsiveness valued? How do new ideas bubble up from
  those close to customers and markets? What are the
  mechanisms whereby best practices, new ideas, and
  learning are shared?

- *Perspective:* What are your organization's history and values? How do they create value for customers? How do
  people work with each other? What is the lens through
  which new opportunities are viewed?

# 3

---

# Unit Structure

I MAGINE AN ORGANIZATION made up of a variety of three-dimensional shapes. Rectangular blocks represent the functions: manufacturing, R&D, and sales and marketing. The spheres are regional offices. Pyramids represent product groups—one for, say, automotive, another for industrial, a third for consumer products. Finally, a series of cubes represents major customers.

The shapes lie scattered on your desk. Your job is to fit the pieces together. Do you place the spheres on top of the blocks so that functions report to the regions? Or should it be the other way around, with the regions subordinate to the functions? Maybe you should organize by product, with separate units set up to serve specific markets. You play with the different combinations in your hands. How to decide . . .

This is the most obvious—and vexing—problem of organization design: grouping work units according to specific criteria. A study by the Conference Board came to the following conclusion:

> There appears to be little evidence to suggest which of the
> [various] organizational formats would be best to assure the

business' overall success, or even why it uses a specific format. This is largely due to the fact that the role of organization in regard to a business unit's success, or in the choice of which structure to use, is intertwined with a large number of other important factors. These include the strategy of the business, the quality of its leadership and work force, the excellence of its products, and its administrative heritage; also, the "fit" or alignment among important organization design elements such as structure, business systems, staffing, rewards, and tasks.[1]

In other words, the problem is too difficult. There is no clear pathway to a solution.

This chapter offers an approach to solve the organization structure problem. The solution will be derived through analysis of the first of our four Cs: customer definition. Using an "outside-in" approach, we will start by designing units that work most closely with customers and markets; then we will progressively move inside the firm to create subunits that define the operating core. As you will see, responsiveness is the critical objective for units close to the customer; economic efficiency and cost control are more important for units in the operating core.

## WHO IS YOUR CUSTOMER?

A great deal has been written in the strategy and marketing literature on the importance of creating customer value. In our everyday language, we think of a customer as someone who buys goods or services. But we have recently witnessed an explosion in the definition of a customer.

In popular marketing textbooks, students are taught that a customer is any person or organizational unit that plays a role in the consummation of a transaction with the organization. This definition includes buyers, users, and payers. For example, an office assistant may order office products to be used by fifty people in a department and paid for by a central accounts payable facility. All these entities are customers. The advice to managers: "Look at all your business relationships as if they were customers . . . By viewing everyone as a customer, you fundamentally change the nature of the value proposition that exists between you and the entities with whom you interact."[2]

This theme is echoed in another recent book, *Everyone Is a Customer*: "Today, the term customer not only means the traditional customer but every entity that interacts with you in a significant manner."[3] This claim is repeated in the book *The Customer Is CEO*, which defines a customer as "the recipient of any kind of product or service provided by an organization, a recipient inside or outside."[4] The author adds, "When thinking about which customers to pay attention to, the wisest choice is to cast the net broadly. They are all important."

According to these authors, everyone is a customer of someone else. There are internal customers and external customers: the manufacturing division is a customer of the R&D division, and the marketing department is a customer of manufacturing. In some accounts, employees are customers of management.

Although people may like being called customers—to foster their sense of importance and self-worth—following this well-intentioned fad can lead to an unintended, but insidious, outcome. *By labeling everyone a customer, the organization becomes confused about its purpose and whom it is designed to serve.* If everyone is a customer, then no one is—and focus on the real customer is lost.

We made this mistake at Harvard Business School in the mid-1990s when a new administration began telling our students that they were customers. In hindsight, the result was predictable: as paying "customers," students demanded that their professors respond promptly to their preferences. Professors and courses had become products that students were purchasing: if customers were unhappy, they reasoned, the product should be changed. Militant demands displaced an environment of mutual respect and shared learning. Needless to say, the practice of telling students they were customers was quickly stopped. (I will have more to say later in this chapter about who the real customer is.)

In fact, the customer is too important to follow the practice of calling everyone a customer. As managers at GE have stated, "Customers are seen for what they are—the lifeblood of a company. Customers' vision of their needs and the company's view become identical, and every effort of every man and woman in the company is focused on satisfying those needs."[5]

Accordingly, the most critical decision in designing any organization is deciding who the *primary* customer is: the person or group that the organization is designed to serve. All significant structures and systems should be configured to ensure that the firm delivers superior value to these (and only these) customers (see figure 3-1). Making this critical decision involves two steps.

**FIGURE 3-1**

**Lever 1: Unit Structure**

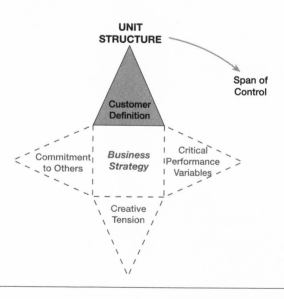

## Step 1: Identify Your Constituents

The first step is to identify all the constituents of an organization. From this set of constituents, managers must choose their primary customer—and organize accordingly.

A *constituent* is a person or group that receives utility from the value creation process of the organization and transacts routinely with the organization through markets. Note that I have limited the definition of a constituent (and ultimately a customer) to include only those who transact with the firm through markets. As a result, this analysis considers only organizations whose customers have choices. I include business firms, nonprofit organizations, and universities; however, I exclude government agencies (in which service provision is mandated by law) as well as monopolies (in which customers have no real alternatives).[6] Also excluded are internal business functions (e.g., human resources and information technology) unless they operate in a true market setting—that is, they are run as profit centers and users can choose to outsource or select an alternative service provider.[7]

Let's look at each of these conditions in turn.

The first condition states that a constituent finds value in the firm's outputs. Who satisfies this definition? Consider two firms providing products to a neighborhood pharmacy: a pharmaceutical company selling prescription drugs, and a consumer products company selling personal care products such as shampoo and beauty aids.

A consumer filling a medical prescription or purchasing face cream would certainly qualify as a constituent: utility is received from the medication, which alleviates a health problem, or the face cream, which enhances skin care. But other individuals and groups also satisfy our definition: pharmacy chains, distributors, hospitals, physicians, and research scientists all benefit in one way or another from the products of these two firms.

FIGURE 3-2

**Market Constituents for a Pharmaceutical Firm**

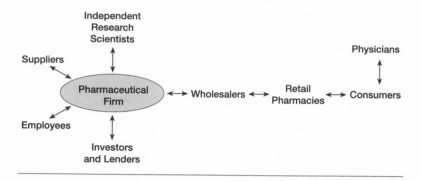

To meet the second condition, a constituent must transact routinely with the firm through markets. Consumers clearly satisfy this condition. But do pharmacies, distributors, hospitals, physicians, and scientists also meet this second condition?

To answer this question we must recognize that there are several markets that are important to the success of organizations. Let's consider the pharmaceutical firm. In its product and service markets, the list of constituents includes consumers, pharmacists, retail pharmacy stores, wholesalers, and distributors. But we should also include clinical physicians and independent research scientists, who transact through knowledge markets. And we must also add shareholders and lenders, who participate through financial markets, and employees in labor markets. All these individuals, groups, and firms are constituents (figure 3-2). But who is the primary customer?

## Step 2: Based on Your Strategy, Determine Your Primary Customer

Organizations can be designed effectively to serve only one master. Accordingly, the pharmaceutical and consumer products companies are designed very differently to serve different customers. Other constituents, important as they may be to the firm's success, are treated differently.

The consumer products firm has identified retail consumers as its primary customer. As a result, the firm emphasizes consumer preference feedback, focus groups, product development, and intensive retail marketing programs. Hospitals, pharmacies, and research scientists are managed as constituents; efforts are made to ensure only that they feel fairly treated in their transactions with the firm.

The pharmaceutical company has chosen a very different path. Because its strategy focuses on basic scientific discovery, it has identified clinical physicians and scientists in the broad research community as its primary customers. Accordingly, the firm is organized to support pure and applied research and the interchange of ideas in the scientific community. Other groups, including retail consumers, are treated as constituents in the process and are managed accordingly.

Identifying the primary customer is not, of course, the end of the story. Managers must still segment the customer market and decide which segments to focus on. For the consumer products company, segmentation focuses on customer demographics: will products be designed to appeal to wealthy, middle-market, or low-income customers? For the pharmaceutical business, segmentation is by therapeutic class: will the firm focus on research related to oncology, psychotherapy, or cardiovascular drugs?

## LEVER 1: UNIT STRUCTURE

Following our outside-in approach, after the primary customer has been defined, the next step is to configure resources into a coherent structure to serve that customer. *Unit structure* is the overall architecture of the organization, which defines unit groupings and the resources that each unit controls. The basic building blocks are market-facing units and operating-core units. *Market-facing units* are clusters of the firm's resources designed to respond directly to the preferences and desires of the primary customer group. *Operating-core units* are the centralized clusters of resources that provide shared products and services to market-facing units.

Market-facing units play a critical role in absorbing information from markets and delivering goods and services. Because of this critical interface, market-facing units need to gather market data about customers, competitors, opportunities, and threats and to deploy that information quickly. Accordingly, *responsiveness* is the key objective for the design of market-facing units.

But, as a rule, responsiveness comes at the cost of *efficiency*. The firm must also create products and services in a way that ensures adequate economic returns. Put simply, managers of the firm must seek a competitive level of profit—a level of economic return that will satisfy shareholders and financial markets. Therefore, managers may choose to create a large and efficient operating core[8] or to outsource key functions.

Managers of operating-core units are responsible for standardizing work processes, applying best practices to the firm's internal operations, and ensuring efficiencies through economies of scale and scope. In some cases, managers may choose to outsource these functions to low-cost service providers that can achieve economies of scale through lower labor costs and the use of advanced technology.

On the one hand, market-facing units require resources if they are to be as responsive as possible to customers. On the other hand, there is a fundamental need to concentrate resources in the operating core to drive economic efficiency. But resources are finite: choices must be made. How should managers allocate scarce resources between market-facing and operating-core units?

## Span of Control

Before proceeding, we now introduce people into the equation and acknowledge that organization structure is essentially a vehicle to place resources in the hands of individual managers and employees. Span of control—one of the four spans that determine span of attention—is traditionally defined as the number of people reporting to an individual manager. For example, a manager's span of control might be seven or ten, representing the number of subordinates reporting directly to that individual.[9]

Here, I adopt a broader definition of span of control. Instead of focusing only on the number of people who report to a manager, I will focus on the *total resources* under a manager's direct control.[10] Thus, for our purposes, *span of control* represents the range of resources for which a manager is given decision rights and held accountable for performance. These resources certainly include people but also encompass balance sheet assets such as accounts receivable, inventory, buildings, and equipment, as well as intangible resources such as trademarks and proprietary processes, customer lists, dealer networks, and brand equity.

At this point it is important to emphasize that span of control—like other spans to be presented in later chapters—focuses on the *vantage point of an individual manager*. For any manager, span of control answers the question, "What resources do I have at my disposal to get the job done?"

To answer this question, span of control can fall anywhere within a range from wide to narrow. A manager with a wide span of control has decision rights, and is accountable, for an extensive number of people, physical assets, distribution facilities, marketing programs, and information systems—in other words, an entire business. A manager with a narrow span of control, by contrast, may have relatively few resources at her disposal.

**FIGURE 3-3**

## Span of Control Design Slider

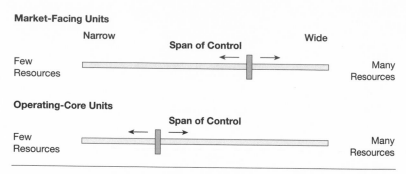

"What Resources Do I Control?"

**Market-Facing Units**

**Operating-Core Units**

We can depict the width of span of control by means of a "slider" similar to the adjustment controls found on a sound mixer (figure 3-3). Using this slider, you can adjust span of control from narrow (few resources) to wide (many resources) for each individual and unit within an organization.

Market-facing managers naturally want a wide span of control to maximize customer responsiveness. They want control of marketing and sales, production, new product development, and so on. However, as the span of control of market-facing units widens, duplication of functions becomes inevitable. As a result, cost efficiencies derived from economies of scale and scope are sacrificed.

Operating-core managers find themselves in the opposite camp. They want to centralize and consolidate operations to drive economies of scale and efficiently share best practices. However, allocating resources to these groups—which are shielded from competitive markets in the operating core of the organization—weaken responsiveness to the primary customer.

To solve this dilemma, managers must ask two questions:

1. What product and service attributes do our primary customers value most?

2. How can we deploy organizational resources to deliver customer value in a way that creates sufficient economic returns?

Strategies that appeal to customer desires for local product formulations, high service levels, or customization tilt the balance toward responsiveness. These strategies require a wide span of control for market-facing managers, who are uniquely informed about how to create customer value. For firms following these strategies, operating-core managers are given a relatively narrow span of control. Efficiencies are traded for enhanced responsiveness.

By contrast, strategies that appeal to customers' desire for low price, consistent brand standards, or advanced technology will tilt the balance in the opposite direction—toward specialization and cost efficiencies. Managers of specialized operating-core units possess both the knowledge and the capability to deliver value on these attributes. Accordingly, the span of control of operating-core managers is widened. They are given the resources needed to standardize, drive economies of scale, and embed the latest technology and quality practices in products and services. Responsiveness to individual customer demands is reduced: market-facing managers are given a relatively narrow span of control.

## FIVE ARCHETYPES OF UNIT STRUCTURE

We can now apply the concept of span of control to describe five structural design archetypes:

- Low price

- Local value creation

- Global standard of excellence

- Dedicated service relationship

- Expert knowledge

Each configuration reflects a unique way to create customer value and economic returns.

Of course, there are many permutations and combinations of these pure types, and many firms will attempt to form bridges between them. Nevertheless, these five configurations establish a comprehensive framework for the design choices facing senior managers. Later chapters address how managers deal with the inevitable complexity that arises when they combine attributes from these pure types to create more complicated structures.

The following discussion assumes that managers have identified their primary customer. The job now is to understand how to deploy resources to ensure the implementation of a strategy that creates value for these customers.

## Low-Price Configuration

As the name suggests, managers choose the *low-price* configuration when they have decided to target customers who place primary value on product price. The value proposition may include a combination of standardized features and quality levels, but the foundation of this strategy is the customer who values consistency in product attributes and low price.

This strategy can be found in virtually all industries—fast food restaurants, retail outlets, financial services, and airlines. Firms in this category include Wal-Mart, TJX stores (Marshalls and T.J. Maxx), Dell Computer, Vanguard (mutual funds), Amazon.com, JetBlue Airways and Southwest Airlines, and category killers such as Staples (office supplies) and The Home Depot (building supplies).

Although this strategy has mass appeal, low prices typically yield low profit margins. Therefore, for this strategy to be profitable, senior managers must ensure both internal efficiencies and high volume turnover. To achieve these margins, operating-core managers are given control of all resources that contribute to economies of scale and scope. Accordingly, span of control is very wide for managers of internal operating functions such as procurement, manufacturing, store operations, logistics, R&D, marketing, and so on.

Units are grouped by function or work process, and virtually all internal services are consolidated into the operating core. Large-scale operating-core units are expected to supply inputs to market-facing units efficiently and cost effectively. Managers in charge of operating-core functions attempt to bring as many overlapping resources as possible under one roof, eliminating redundancies, encouraging specialization, and ensuring that resources are deployed to their highest and best use.

As these firms become larger and cover wider geographical areas, their distribution networks—the point of contact with the customer—typically are organized on a regional basis. For example, the retail outlets of most large superstore chains are grouped by region, with separate units created to serve the northeast, central, and western regions of the United States.

However, these regional groupings still focus on achieving economies of scale and efficiency. Therefore, the span of control of regional store managers—the market-facing units—is very narrow. Managers of the operating-core functions retain decision rights over store layouts, menus, merchandise displays, prices, uniforms, signage, and so on. Store managers are given few degrees of freedom: they are evaluated on how well they implement the standards laid down by the powerful operating-core functions and the speed with which they can process transactions to generate revenue.

Sometimes, execution of a low-price strategy requires local store managers to coordinate inputs such as food ingredients and hourly labor in a fast food franchise. Even in these cases,

FIGURE 3-4

## Organization Chart for a Low-Price Retailer

however, store operators are given only a marginally wider span of control. The operating core still tightly controls brand and format consistency. Ingredients are purchased at a regional level. Human resource professionals based in the regions, who report directly to centrally managed core functions, are responsible for labor hiring. Store managers are accountable only for achieving wage rate and hourly utilization targets.

A typical organization chart for a retailer following a low-price strategy is illustrated in figure 3-4.

However, figure 3-4 does not do justice to the unique resource allocation choices embedded in a low-price structure. Figure 3-5 provides a more accurate depiction of the relative resources controlled by market-facing and operating-core units. Here, the area allocated to each unit represents its relative span of control.

As figure 3-5 illustrates, even though the retail stores are the main point of interaction for the customer, the span of control of store managers is extremely limited. By contrast, the span of control is much greater for managers who oversee the operating-core functions, where both knowledge and the capability to create low-price value for the primary customer reside.

## Local Value Creation Configuration

Rather than offer standardized products and low prices, some firms choose to compete by tailoring products and services to

**FIGURE 3-5**

## Span of Control: Retailer Low-Price Configuration

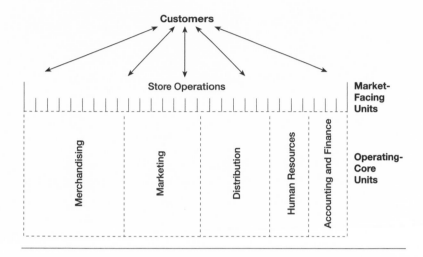

the needs or tastes of customers in particular geographic regions. For these firms, managers typically choose to organize using a *local value creation* structure.

For companies tailoring products and services by region, it is not sufficient to simply import a standard product and change packaging or translate product manuals into local languages. Differing consumer preferences, laws, or engineering standards may result in the need to offer significantly different versions of the same product. For example, international food manufacturers such as Nestlé adjust product formulations to accommodate local preferences for spices and sweets. Global accounting firms such as PricewaterhouseCoopers hire locally trained accountants who are familiar with country-specific accounting standards and tax codes. Automakers customize their product offerings to reflect local driving customs (left or right side of the road), road width (Japan levies higher taxes for wider cars), and customer preferences regarding styling and interior features.

For these firms, a significant portion of value creation must be located close to the customer. As a result, many functions that would otherwise be centralized in the operating core—procurement, R&D, manufacturing, and marketing—are pushed out to the regions. Thus, these functions are duplicated in each local market.

Because of the need to gather, process, and act on local information, the span of control allocated to managers heading up these regional units is typically wide. The resources within their control include factories, R&D laboratories, marketing and sales divisions, distribution networks, and administration functions. In fact, these organizations are usually constituted as full legal entities, with their own charters, assets and liabilities, financial statements, tax returns, and other government filings.

The role of centralized corporate functions is correspondingly diminished. With the majority of resources pushed out to the market-facing regional businesses, the center retains control of only a limited number of core operating functions, such as corporate marketing, basic research, and corporate accounting.

Figure 3-6 illustrates what a local value creation configuration looks like for an international food company. From a customer's point of view, products and services reflect local tastes or product requirements. From an organization design perspective, the span of control in the regional units is wide; the residual span of control found in the operating core is relatively narrow.

Of course, for regional businesses to be profitable, customers must value—and be willing to pay for—local customization. The duplication of operations in each regional unit, coupled with the move away from the efficiencies that might be achieved by centralized operating-core functions, results in a configuration that is inherently high cost. For the business to be profitable and earn adequate returns, prices must be commensurately higher.

FIGURE 3-6

## Span of Control: International Food Company
## Local Value Creation Configuration

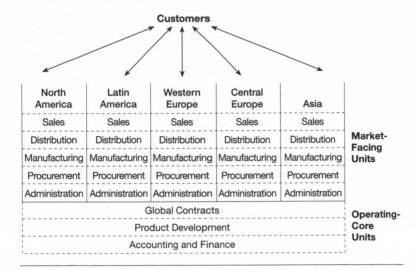

At Procter & Gamble, management justified the costly duplication of its local value creation structure as follows: "The impact of unique consumer perceptions or characteristics of the local marketplace more than offsets the cost-effectiveness of simplification and standardization. A good understanding of the consumer often dictates different products and different marketing strategies."[11]

Political considerations can also cause managers to allocate resources to regional market-facing units. For example, in industries where the primary customer is a government department or nationalized industry, firms may be required to add a significant amount of local content as a condition of winning contracts. In these cases, the product is often less customized, but the result is similar. The span of control vested in market-facing units is relatively high (although, in this case, the market-facing units may rely more heavily on corporate operating-core functions for shared services and basic manufacturing and engineering platforms).

## Global Standard of Excellence Configuration

Rather than offer low price or regionalized products, some firms choose to compete by offering products and services that possess unique features that are both valued by customers and difficult for competitors to copy. For these firms, excellence in product design, technology, or brand attributes is at the heart of their value proposition. These firms aspire to set a *global standard of excellence* in product features or brand awareness or both.

In this customer segment, value is created by products that offer the latest and most advanced technologies (e.g., software, robotics, power generation systems) or strong brand attributes (e.g., consumer goods, credit cards). Firms such as Intel, Boeing, American Express, Estée Lauder, and General Electric follow this strategy.

To support and continually upgrade the superiority of their products, these firms typically make large-scale investments in technology, R&D, and marketing to build brand equity. Yet in any specific region or country, the number of customers willing to pay a premium for product or service excellence may be relatively small. Therefore, these firms tend to define their target customer on a global basis to amortize these expenditures over as large a customer base as possible. Customers are buying—and benefiting from the attributes of—the same product no matter where they may be located: the purchaser of a power generating plant wants to receive the benefits of the latest engineering technology applied anywhere in the world; a credit card consumer desires the global accessibility and prestige of the branded credit card.

Firms offering this value proposition configure their market-facing units by global product family rather than by region or function. In this structure, a stand-alone unit is given responsibility for developing and marketing a specific product on a worldwide basis. All the resources required to meet customer needs and compete effectively are subsumed within the product unit. On a traditional organization chart, each product family gets its own box.

There are two reasons for this choice. First, organizing by global product family allows firms to create economies of scale in R&D, brand marketing, and specialized production technologies. All resources of the unit are dedicated to one product family and can be centrally organized and managed. Regional redundancies and overlaps are eliminated, and scarce resources can be pooled to create technologically advanced products and strong brands.

Second, in a multiproduct firm where products have different production technologies or primary customers, separate product divisions can focus attention on and become knowledgeable about a single product or product family. Within each product division, all employees—whether from marketing, sales, production, or R&D—can devote their full attention to understanding a particular technology or brand. In this way, they become more responsive to customers, emerging opportunities, and competitive actions.

For this reason, the new CEO of Gillette (since acquired by Procter & Gamble) moved smaller product categories such as shaving cream and deodorants out of the dominant razor division, where they were the "ignored stepchild," and created a new division to house them where they would receive more focus.[12] Similarly, after a decade of growth and dominance in the mobile-phone market, Nokia reorganized its operations into four business groups—mobile phones, multimedia, networks, and enterprise solutions—to ensure that opportunities in these newly emerging markets would receive sufficient attention.

From a customer's perspective, the firm looks like figure 3-7.

As with the regional design, this configuration places a disproportionate span of control in the hands of managers of market-

**FIGURE 3-7**

### Span of Control: International Manufacturing Company Global Standard of Excellence Configuration

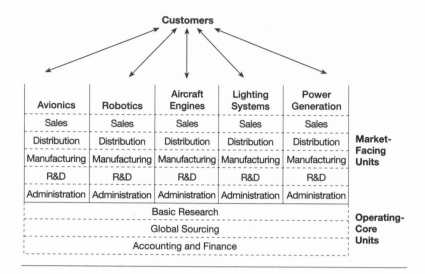

| Avionics | Robotics | Aircraft Engines | Lighting Systems | Power Generation | |
|---|---|---|---|---|---|
| Sales | Sales | Sales | Sales | Sales | |
| Distribution | Distribution | Distribution | Distribution | Distribution | **Market-Facing Units** |
| Manufacturing | Manufacturing | Manufacturing | Manufacturing | Manufacturing | |
| R&D | R&D | R&D | R&D | R&D | |
| Administration | Administration | Administration | Administration | Administration | |
| Basic Research | | | | | **Operating-Core Units** |
| Global Sourcing | | | | | |
| Accounting and Finance | | | | | |

facing units, but in this case the market-facing units are product divisions. The span of control in the centralized operating core—primarily shared services functions—is correspondingly diminished.

Again, given the high degree of investment spending and redundancies created by separate marketing, R&D, production, and distribution units within each product division, it is usually necessary to charge higher prices to generate adequate margins. Therefore, for this strategy to succeed, customers must appreciate and be willing to pay for the large investments made to create value and differentiate products and services.

## Dedicated Service Relationship Configuration

The *dedicated service relationship* configuration is found when firms have decided to compete by offering important customers a long-term service relationship. Products and services are not merely one-time sales events but instead are part of a continuing relationship aimed at generating solutions that have enduring value to the customer. Long-term customer satisfaction and responsiveness to customer needs are the bases for differentiation.

Information technology companies such as Siebel Systems, SAP, and IBM follow this strategy, as do strategy consulting firms such as McKinsey and BCG, and investment banking firms such as Lehman Brothers. As an advertisement by software company SAP declared, "Your Customers Expect Your Entire Enterprise To Revolve Around Them."[13]

In this configuration, separate units are created for each key customer or customer group. At IBM, for example, the thirty-eight thousand people in the software group have been clustered into twelve major industry groups: automobiles, consumer goods, financial services, healthcare, telecommunications, and so on. In this design, each group is expected to focus on and develop solutions to the unique problems of its customer group.[14]

Span of control in this design is split relatively evenly between managers of market-facing units and managers of operating-core units. The operating core is typically responsible for basic R&D, product platforms, manufacturing, and corporate marketing. The market-facing units—often organized on a team basis—are responsible for working with the customer to tailor the basic product or service to fit that customer's needs.

These market-facing units control all the resources—a dedicated sales team, system engineering, logistics, and after-sales support—that are needed to customize and deliver products that are uniquely suited to the customer's specific needs.

Accordingly, the market-facing units have their own units dedicated to product customization, customer marketing, and pre- and post-service. At IBM, this team approach is called "four in a box," referring to the customer teams that represent corporate account management, the services division, the software unit, and the research lab.[15] Members of these units interact extensively to solve problems and improve processes to achieve a common goal of customer satisfaction.

For this type of organization to be profitable, a customer or customer group must be significant—both in absolute terms and relative to the total customer base—and must have unique product or service requirements that can best be met through customization of products, delivery channels, and service. As in the previous examples, because of the cost of redundancy and customization, this is a relatively high-cost configuration. Accordingly, the customer must be willing to pay a higher price for value received if this strategy is to be profitable. Figure 3-8 illustrates this concept.

## Expert Knowledge Configuration

The final configuration is the most unusual and least frequently encountered. Nevertheless, it is interesting for two reasons.

**FIGURE 3-8**

**Span of Control: Computer Company
Dedicated Service Relationship Configuration**

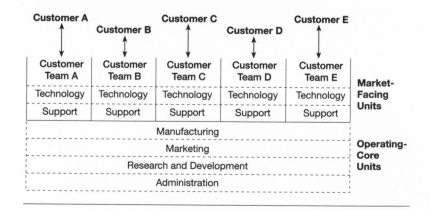

First, this is how Harvard Business School—where I work—is organized. More importantly, however, this configuration underlines the importance of a distinction introduced at the beginning of the chapter that we now revisit: the distinction between a customer and a constituent, and the effect of this distinction on organization design.

The *expert knowledge* configuration looks very much like the low-price configuration. However, instead of organizing resources by work process or function, units are grouped by knowledge specialty. The reasons are familiar: organizing by function or knowledge encourages specialization and technical excellence.[16] In this configuration, however, customers reside in knowledge markets rather than product markets.

Consider Harvard Business School, a small but complex organization of two hundred professors and one thousand support staff, administrators, and research assistants. At Harvard, as with most university graduate schools, the primary customer is not the student but rather academics in outside universities, who rely on the school to create and share knowledge.

The research and course development work of the Harvard professors represents the face of the school to our customers—outside academics. Thus, the school is organized by knowledge specialty rather than by either teaching program (e.g., MBA program, executive program, etc.) or work process (e.g., admissions, student placement, etc.). On campus, professors sit together grouped by specialty: accounting, finance, marketing, organization behavior, strategy, and so on. All other administrative functions that relate to teaching programs and student affairs are functionally (and physically) separate.

This somewhat unusual configuration is not limited to the professional environments of universities and hospitals. It can also be found in any business that chooses to compete in knowledge markets and some that compete in financial markets. For example, hedge funds that target sophisticated pension fund advisers, such as Bain Capital's Sankaty Advisors, use the expert knowledge configuration to create separate units by knowledge specialty (e.g., autos, chemicals, media, technology, etc.).[17]

Carried to the extreme, managers of some of theses financial investment firms may decide that their primary customers are their "star" portfolio managers. The strategy of these firms is to identify, attract, and retain unusually skilled investment experts who can consistently generate above-market returns (and who are, therefore, actively sought after in financial labor markets). The visibility of these highly ranked experts will then attract revenue-generating clients to the firm.[18]

Consider again the pharmaceutical company discussed at the beginning of this chapter. Expert research knowledge and specialized work processes differentiate the firm; scientists and clinical physicians in research hospitals and universities represent the primary customer. An organization chart for this pharmaceutical firm is shown in figure 3-9.

In traditional terms, this giant firm, employing more than fifty thousand people, is organized by function or work process. But as you have seen before, a traditional organization chart is conceptually deficient because it shows all functions to be equal. In fact, research and development activities predominate and are

**FIGURE 3-9**

**Functional Organization Chart for a Pharmaceutical Company**

**FIGURE 3-10**

## Span of Control: Pharmaceutical Company Expert Knowledge Configuration

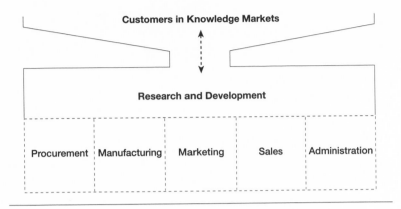

tightly linked to outside knowledge markets. New ideas and intellectual capital flow back and forth freely between the firm and outside researchers by means of professional associations, conferences, publications, and a strong network of formal and informal professional relationships with universities and researchers around the world.

Figure 3-10 tells the story more accurately: one critical function—R&D—dominates the value creation process. In the eyes of customers (scientists and clinical physicians in research hospitals and universities), this function alone creates the unique value that underlies the value proposition. Accordingly, the span of control allocated to the market-facing R&D unit relative to other units is very wide. The operating core is allocated a relatively narrow span of control.

For these types of organizations to survive, it is essential that customers in knowledge markets—who do not actually pay the bills—have the ability to influence the constituents who supply the revenue. In the pharmaceutical company, for example, the work of the outside research community and clinical professionals—

validating the efficacy of new drugs and communicating through professional publications and interactions with regulatory authorities—influences physician prescription patterns and the ultimate spending choices of healthcare providers and patients. Similarly, Harvard Business School relies on academics in universities around the world to require their students to purchase Harvard case studies and to recommend that their graduates apply to Harvard Business School programs.

Constituents are willing to fund these organizations, which are organized primarily to benefit others, only because there is no market-based relationship between product price and the value received by users. In a pharmaceutical company, for example, the price for a new cancer drug is not determined either by the cost to develop and manufacture the compound or by the potential value to the patient; instead, pricing is determined by the ability to pay of the constituents involved: healthcare insurers, corporate sponsors, regulators, and so on. (In fact, the cost of manufacturing drugs is often less than 5 percent of selling price, leading to the tongue-in-cheek observation that drug production is more profitable than the manufacture of U.S. dollar bills.) Similarly, for graduate education, the price of an MBA degree bears no relationship to the cost of providing the service or the value to the student. Instead, price is determined by limits on the willingness of constituents (students, parents, government agencies, etc.) to pay.

Because of this lack of market-based price pressure, cost efficiency is generally a low priority for expert knowledge organizations. Senior managers adjust the span of control to maximize responsiveness to knowledge markets, with relatively little regard for efficiency. Experts in the market-facing units (professors, research scientists, physicians) are allocated all available resources, subject only to the constraint of revenue intake from the constituents who actually pay the bills.

## Cycling Back to Strategy

The expert knowledge archetype underlines the importance of identifying the primary customer and organizing resources to serve that customer. Consider two successful global credit card companies. Each company offers a well-known branded credit card through retail banks around the world. Constituents of these two companies include consumers, merchants, member banks, cobranding alliance partners, and electronic payment processing organizations.

Although on the surface these two companies look very similar, each has made a different strategic choice in defining its primary customer. This choice has determined how each has structured its business.

One of these companies—let's call it company A—offers a low-price value proposition to its primary customer group: global banks and corporate card sponsors. To build brand equity, company A appeals to consumers and corporate users around the world through large-scale global marketing campaigns. Advertising programs emphasize global acceptance and cobranding with other product and service providers. Merchants, regional member banks, and alliance partners are not primary customers; instead, they are constituents in the value creation process.

With its decision to compete through low price, global acceptance, and high volume, company A has adopted the low-price configuration to achieve economies of scale. Centralized operating-core functions include new product development, marketing, alliance management, and payment processing. Span of control for these functions is very wide. Market-facing units in countries around the world have a relatively narrow span of control—limited to minimal interfaces with regional member banks and the coordination of centrally developed and globally consistent advertising campaigns.

The second of these firms, company B, has chosen a different path. This firm has identified regional member banks as its primary customer group. Company B works closely with member banks in countries around the world to offer them a value proposition based on local customization and cobranding. This approach relies on member banks to, in turn, push card usage with their own retail customers. For both firms, retail consumers are constituents.

Unlike its competitor, company B has chosen to organize by region. Because this firm has adopted a local value creation configuration, the role of market-facing units is to be as responsive as possible to the needs of regional member banks. Each regional unit has its own new product development and marketing resources, and advertising and new product development are customized by region. Only global marketing (a relatively minor function) and payment processing are centralized. As a result of the duplication of regional functions, the prices of company B's card and services are higher than those of company A.

Of course, the choice of primary customer, like any strategic choice, entails risk. This risk was highlighted through the 1990s and early 2000s when large auditing firms chose corporate executives as their primary customer. All other groups, including shareholders and regulators, were treated as constituents. In attempting to respond to the needs of their corporate executive clients, partners and managers of the powerful regional audit offices, with wide spans of control, allowed liberal accounting practices to go unreported. Today, following highly publicized financial frauds and failures, new central oversight structures have been installed in these firms. This change has been driven by a new recognition that shareholders—represented by boards of directors—must become the primary customer group. Not surprisingly, with this change in focus these firms have reorganized from a local value creation configuration to a more centralized global standard of excellence configuration.

Labeling everyone a customer yields confusion and results in a peanut butter approach to resource allocation—spreading the same amount of resources unthinkingly over all organizational units. In a well-known manufacturer of home renovation products, there was confusion about the primary customer: was it the retail consumer or the independent dealer network? As a result of uncertainty concerning strategy and span of control, resources were allocated evenly across all functions. Critical functions—notably R&D—became underfunded. Not surprisingly, this firm lost ground to more focused competitors that marshaled resources to meet the needs of one primary customer group.[19]

As these examples remind us, choosing the primary customer is one of the fundamental decisions of business strategy. It is easy to argue that everyone is a customer and that managers should therefore offer everything to everyone. In an ideal world, we might like this to be possible. But in a world of constraints—both of resources and of management attention—attempting to be all things to all people can lead to only one inevitable conclusion: there is no clear strategy.

### Changing Strategy

Of course, strategies do and must change over time. A business strategy that was effective in the past will, at some point in the future, prove ineffective. The question is whether such a change must precipitate a crisis.

Consider McDonald's, the world's largest franchise restaurant company. For more than forty years, McDonald's focused its business on aggressive growth of its franchise concept. By 2003, McDonald's had grown to thirty-one thousand restaurants around the world, including thirteen thousand in the United States. Of these restaurants, 85 percent were owned by franchisees. Over a period of decades, the company was opening as many as seventeen hundred new stores per year. This was called, by some, "the largest retail expansion boom in the history of the world."[20]

Jeffrey Bradach, in a study of franchise organizations, described the McDonald's strategy:

> The growth in the number of units far exceeded the growth in the revenue generated by existing units . . . Revenue and profit increases—which had been monumental through the 1960s, 1970s, and 1980s—[came] almost exclusively from unit additions. The tight relationship between adding units and chain growth suggests that the business format itself is the product, one that is essentially "sold" with the opening of each new outlet. In fact, it is precisely this product— the business format—that a franchisee buys when joining a chain.[21]

To fuel growth, McDonald's was organized to support its primary customer: real estate developers and multisite franchise owners who controlled valuable real estate. It should come as no surprise that McDonald's was configured as a low-price company with a very large and powerful centralized operating core. Powerful operating-core functions tightly controlled brand concept, franchising, real estate development, procurement, menus, and food preparation. As suggested in figure 3-5, store operators were given a very narrow span of control.

During the 1990s, however, consumers—a critical constituent in the business formula—tired of McDonald's standardized, low-price fare. By 2003, the business posted losses for the first time in history and was forced to close seven hundred restaurants and suspend operations in three countries.[22] Managers were confronted with changing tastes: consumers wanted more varied menus—both increased choice and sensitivity to regional food.

In response to changes in its markets, McDonald's made two fundamental decisions. First, top managers changed their strategy by redefining their primary customer, moving away from the past focus on real estate developers. As McDonald's CEO stated, "The new boss at McDonald's is the consumer."[23]

Second, McDonald's reorganized to respond more effectively to its newly declared customer. Instead of following the centralized functional configuration typical of low-price companies, it reorganized by region to a local value creation configuration. For the first time, regional market-facing units were given resources to customize local menus and store layouts. As a result, some local franchisees installed wood paneling in dining rooms, created separate seating areas with sofas and coffee tables, introduced custom-ordered sandwiches, and hired tuxedoed doormen to greet customers.[24] New performance measures were also instituted to increase the accountability of franchisees and their store operators (I discuss this topic in detail in chapter 4).

Of course, McDonald's faces the same challenges experienced by any company that reorganizes to reflect a change in strategy. Lost efficiencies must be recovered through higher prices. Customers must be willing to recognize the new value added through local customization and must be willing to pay increased prices. Coca-Cola is feeling the same pressures. A one-product company until 1982 (with the launch of Diet Coke), Coca-Cola now manages more than two hundred local brands around the world, and the number continues to grow.[25]

A different, but equally profound, metamorphosis has occurred at Microsoft. During its heady growth years, Microsoft was organized principally by knowledge group—following an expert knowledge configuration. Span of control was tilted heavily to the product development technology groups, which received the lion's share of resources. A separate companywide sales group was responsible for revenue generation. Profit and loss was calculated only at the highest levels of the company.

When the software market matured and growth peaked in 2003, Microsoft reorganized and adopted the global standard of excellence configuration. The new structure created seven product divisions—Windows, server software, mobile software, office software, video games, business software, and Internet service—each with its own product development, sales and marketing, finance, and other production functions. Each product division is now headed by a general manager who has profit and loss accountability. This new unit structure allows the company to delegate resources and decision making to managers who are closer to end-user customers. Microsoft hopes to combine this increased market awareness with its strong technological capability to create products that are the standards of excellence in each of the seven identified business units.

For the first time, Microsoft's new structure allows general managers to make their own choices about how to allocate resources to achieve their financial targets and strategic goals. Each group has been given the decision rights to make tradeoffs between headcount, marketing expenditures, and acquisitions. In the past, these decisions were reserved for Microsoft's CEO.[26]

## Drawing the Boundary Between Responsiveness and Efficiency

Just as an architect must balance tradeoffs when allocating space among rooms, organization design is necessarily a tradeoff between responsiveness and efficiency. Some archetypes (e.g., local value creation) tilt the balance toward responsiveness; others (e.g., low price) tilt the balance toward efficiency. But this is not the end of the story. Within each archetype, a decision must be made about where to draw the line between market-facing units (created for responsiveness) and operating-core units (created for efficiency).

Within the global standard of excellence configuration, for example, managers in different firms may draw the line at different points. In one firm, there may be little sharing of resources between business units. This is the case, for example, at Estée Lauder, where each of the various cosmetics brands (Origins, Clinique, Estée Lauder) not only competes with the others for shelf space but also has its own marketing, finance, manufacturing, distribution, and product development units. Only procurement is centralized, with economies of sourcing shared among the different business units.[27] This approach is illustrated in figure 3-11a.

Other firms may place more emphasis on achieving economies of scale and scope by sharing platforms and key processes, leaving it up to the separate business units to rework or customize products and services as needed for their particular markets and customers (figure 3-11b).

At Intel, for example, all businesses share the same manufacturing capability and sales force.[28] Honda follows what it calls a "glocalization" strategy—centralized R&D and consistency of corporate culture, but with most design decisions made at the local country level. Engines and other key technologies are developed in Japan, but exterior designs and cabin features are tailored to local markets. Accordingly, the exterior sheet metal designs for Accord models are different in the United States, Europe, and Japan. Even within North America, different models of the Acura are offered in Canada and the United States to reflect differences in national demographics.[29]

General Motors is moving in the same direction. GM has historically been organized using a local value creation design—allowing different countries to design and engineer their cars for local markets. To obtain global economies of scale in engineering,

FIGURE 3-11

# Span of Control: Drawing the Boundary Between Responsiveness and Efficiency

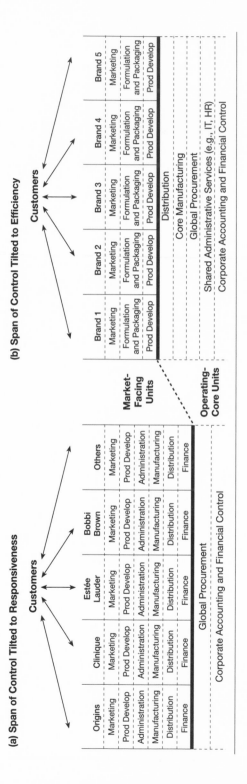

(a) Span of Control Tilted to Responsiveness

(b) Span of Control Tilted to Efficiency

production, and design, GM began in 2002 to centralize key operations by moving selected brands and platforms to a global standard of excellence configuration. To preserve local appeal, regions will continue to modify styling for local tastes.[30]

## Separating Units to Serve Different Customers

It is tempting to think that managers can endlessly mix and match, blending attributes from the different archetypes to create designs that reflect unique aspects of their strategy. But an important corollary emerges from the foregoing analysis: organizations that choose to serve more than one primary customer must create separate, independent organizations structured to serve each different customer.

In some instances, uniqueness may result from regional differences among customers; in other instances, uniqueness may reflect differing needs for technology or brand attributes. At 3M, for example, a manager explains,

> Each of our forty-five divisions is oriented toward its specific customer base. And each is a business unto itself, with its own general manager, marketing director, technical director, human resources, manufacturing director, and national sales manager. Divisional autonomy allows each unit to focus its energies directly on its customers' particular needs.[31]

At a corporate level, the segregation of businesses by customer is typically reflected by the creation of separate and independent sectors. For example, industrial companies such as Ingersoll-Rand are organized into four sectors, each serving a different primary customer: climate control, industrial solutions, security and safety, and infrastructure.[32] Similarly, it is common for large banks to create separate organizations for their retail and corporate investment activities.

Companies that attempt to mix and match units to serve more than one primary customer often encounter difficulties. At Bausch & Lomb, for example, the fashion-sensitive sunglass business was organized using a global standard of excellence configuration to sell Raybans to retail consumers. By contrast, the contact lens business was organized on a regional basis according to the local value creation configuration to serve local ophthalmologists and optometrists. At the critical market interface, market-facing units in different regions and countries were asked to deal simultaneously with both—very different—sets of customers. As a result, regional managers were forced to split their time and resources, and they struggled to respond to the different needs of these two customer groups. More focused competitors overtook Bausch & Lomb, and financial losses mounted. In the end, the fashion sunglass business was divested and all resources were reorganized to concentrate on the lens care business.

## What about Constituents?

Notwithstanding the importance of primary customers, managers cannot ignore their organization's other constituents. Depending on the business, constituents might include retail consumers, franchise operators, wholesalers and retailers in the supply chain, alliance partners, and shareholders. Many of these constituents are vital to the ongoing success of the firm. Managers must ensure that their needs are satisfied at some minimum threshold level. This is a lower standard of performance than used for customers: for customers, the objective is to maximize; for constituents, the objective is to "satisfice."[33]

When important constituents are outside the value chain—notably those in financial and labor markets—separate functions must be created to satisfy their interests. All large firms therefore create specialized functions, such as treasury and investor relations, to deal with constituents in financial markets, and human relations, to deal with employees and contract negotiations in labor markets. Depending on strategy, some firms may also create specialized regulatory affairs functions (pharmaceutical firms), franchise owner relations functions (hotel management companies), or alumni affairs functions (university business schools).

When constituents are an integral part of the value chain—for example, supplying inputs and distributing products—regular business functions such as procurement and distribution can be dedicated to meet their needs. Formal contracts are used to deal with these constituents whenever possible. Legal contracts have the advantage of specifying the terms of trade, so that both sides feel fairly dealt with, and of limiting the need for continuing management oversight. By relying on contracts to ensure that the needs of constituents are met, managers can focus their energies on growth in their primary customer markets. Thus, at McDonald's, detailed legal agreements set out all aspects of operations—menus, food quality, store signage and layout, and required financial reporting—that existing franchisees must follow. Organizational attention can then be devoted to working with real estate developers and new franchisees.

Similar types of contracts often exist for suppliers and distributors. At GE Appliances, for example, contracts with dealers guarantee next-day delivery if GE's online ordering system is used. Participating dealers no longer have to hold high levels of inventory. In exchange, the dealers commit to several contractual conditions: selling all major GE product categories, ensuring that GE products generate at least 50 percent of sales, and committing to payment by electronic funds transfer within a fixed number of days.[34]

Going one step further, managers may decide to eliminate constituents from the value chain to limit distractions and enhance competitive position. Dell Computer did just this by eliminating wholesalers and dealers from its distribution channel. Instead, Dell sells directly to customers, enhancing its low-cost position.

## Outsourcing

The outsourcing of operating-core functions is often an effective way to lower costs and free scarce management attention. The number of firms outsourcing business functions has increased dramatically over the past decade. Not only are firms outsourcing support functions such as accounting and payroll, but also they are now routinely outsourcing R&D, manufacturing, customer service centers, and sales and marketing.

When managers consider outsourcing, the distinction between primary customer and constituent becomes especially important. Activities that affect constituents can be outsourced with little risk (assuming adequate quality standards and accountability mechanisms are in place). Similarly, some operating-core functions (e.g., manufacturing) and support functions (e.g., accounting) that do not affect customers directly can also be outsourced safely.

Managers must proceed carefully, however, when outsourced activities affect a firm's ability to create value for its primary customer. Consider, for example, an automotive firm like BMW. This company outsources its emergency roadside service to independent firms that operate twenty-four-hour call centers. Problems can arise because the call center company has a different primary customer from that of its client: in fact, the call center's primary customer is BMW, and not the automobile owner on the telephone with a dead battery. Depending on the circumstances, the call center manager may not give the automobile owner the level of attention and resources that BMW would choose to ensure continuing customer loyalty in a difficult situation.

When outsourced activities affect primary customers directly, careful safeguards must be in place to ensure adequate quality and service levels. Moreover, if any activities are strategic in the customer value proposition—that is, important for differentiation and value creation—outsourcing will generally not be considered.

## USING IT TO BALANCE RESPONSIVENESS AND EFFICIENCY

We now come to an important theme that will carry through the remainder of the book: the critical nature of information technology in organization design. Advances in technology have allowed organizations following each of the design archetypes to grow to unprecedented sizes. Wal-Mart, a low-price competitor, employs 1.3 million people; General Electric, a global standard of excellence company, employs 315,000 people; and IBM, now increasingly following a dedicated service relationship strategy, also employs more than 300,000 workers. Organizations of this size and scale would be unimaginable without the information technologies that support them.

Satellite communication, broadband information networks, and electronic data interchanges have fundamentally changed the range of design options available to managers. Consider Otis Elevator's service business. To support a strategy of local responsiveness, the business was historically organized into six regions with more than two hundred fifty branch offices. Each branch was given a wide span of control to manage scheduling, customer communication, and performance monitoring. All key customer information was retained inside the branch, with little coordination from the center. Maintenance mechanics set their own schedules as they juggled routine work with customer service requests.

Over time, lower-cost competitors eroded Otis's competitive position. In response, a new centralized technology solution—

the service management system—was installed to centrally collect customer information, standardize scheduling, communicate to customers and field agents, and monitor performance. This new information system, with its centralization of customer data, allowed senior managers to redesign the organization from a local value creation configuration to a low-price configuration. New scheduling efficiencies lowered costs. In addition, Otis eliminated the entire middle management organization because regional managers—whose primary job was to interface between the branches and the head office—were no longer needed.[35]

Additional efficiencies have been achieved as advanced information technologies have allowed firms to outsource key operating-core functions. BP has outsourced its entire worldwide accounting and finance function to IBM service centers in Tulsa, Lisbon, and Bangalore. These remote service centers process BP's accounts payable, accounts receivable, and financial reporting. IBM also operates most of Procter & Gamble's human resources department and Cisco Systems' after-sales product support.[36]

Electronic information networks that link retail checkout transactions to supplier inventories have allowed low-price configurations to rely heavily on just-in-time inventories, vendor-managed supply chains, and real-time customer purchase and inventory data. Wal-Mart's electronic information system allows suppliers to track the flow of products through distribution centers and Wal-Mart's retail stores, avoiding both excess inventory and stock-outs. This level of real-time tracking is essential in a company where inventory turnover is so fast that 70 percent of retail merchandise is sold before Wal-Mart has paid the suppliers who furnished it.[37]

Some firms have used information technologies to achieve a virtual integration between customer demand and key constituents. By relying on information technology to link suppliers and customers, Dell's direct sales model allowed the company to grow to $12 billion in sales in only thirteen years. CEO Michael Dell comments,

> We turn our inventory over 30 times per year. If you look at the complexity and the diversity of our product line, there's no way we could do that unless we had credible information about what the customer is actually buying. It's a key part of why rivals have had great difficulty competing with Dell. It's not just that we sell direct, it's also our ability to forecast demand—it's both the design of the product and the way the information from the customer flows all the way through manufacturing to our suppliers. If you don't have that tight linkage—the kind of cooperation of information that used to be possible only in vertically integrated companies—then trying to manage to 11 days of inventory would be insane.
>
> The whole idea behind virtual integration is that it lets you meet customers' needs faster and more efficiently than any other model. With vertical integration, you can be an efficient producer—as long as the world isn't changing very much. But virtual integration lets you be efficient and responsive to change at the same time.[38]

By 2004, Dell had upgraded its consolidated global ordering systems so that it was ordering computer components for its manufacturing plants every two hours instead of once a day.[39] In a more disruptive sense, the explosive growth of Amazon.com and eBay has been driven in large part by information technology platforms that seamlessly integrate third-party retailers into Amazon.com and eBay host Web sites. But, following on our earlier discussion, these firms may soon have to contend with a decision about who their primary customer is—consumers or alliance partner retailers—and reorganize accordingly.[40]

## ENSURING FINANCIAL INTEGRITY

Regardless of configuration, every business requires centralized support and shared service functions. Of all these functions, financial control—encompassing accounting, control, and treasury—is the most critical, for four reasons. First, finance is responsible for ensuring that critical constituents in financial markets—shareholders, bondholders, banks, and institutional rating agencies—continue to supply capital to the firm. If the needs of these critical constituents are not met, the firm cannot continue to exist.

Second, the financial control function is responsible for ensuring that adequate information exists inside the firm to support accountability—the foundation of any organization design. Without a strong accounting and finance function, managers could not rely on information for internal planning, control, and accountability, nor could the investment community have confidence in the transparency and integrity of reported performance.

Third, finance is often responsible for enforcing credit policy decisions, ensuring that market-facing managers do not loosen credit standards to boost sales. And, finally, finance is responsible for providing critical shared services such as transaction processing, payroll, and accounts receivable, as well as treasury functions such as cash sweeps.

With increasing size, scope, and geographic diversity of firms, the role of the financial control function has become both more critical and more difficult. The possibility for error increases; and information system breakdowns have the potential to become catastrophic. Because of the importance of the accounting and control function, the design of these units is crucial. But the tension between efficiency and responsiveness again comes to the forefront. Part of the work of these units—

shared accounting services and treasury functions—must be designed for operating scale and efficiency. These functions are largely independent of the chosen structure for market-facing units. But another part of finance's work—supporting line managers in financial analysis, profit planning, and performance management—needs to be oriented to responsiveness. This part of the finance organization must be aligned with the chosen structure of market-facing units.

Earlier, this chapter described the restructuring of Microsoft into seven business units, each headed by a new general manager having profit and loss accountability. As a result of this change—notably the delegation of decision rights to general managers removed from the day-to-day oversight of corporate executives—Microsoft made it a priority to upgrade its finance organization capabilities. Seven new CFOs were hired—one for each business unit—reporting directly to the new general managers. Microsoft was forced to go outside the company to find financial managers having sufficient skills and experience to take on these critically important jobs.[41]

At a minimum, all business units within the firm—whether market-facing or operating-core—should be operating with the same accounting system and chart of accounts. This consistency is necessary to ensure that managers have the tools they need to establish and monitor accountability. Often, however, the accounting systems of the different units are incompatible. This problem is especially acute when structural configurations are changed or new businesses are acquired. As a result, formats may be incompatible, and it may be difficult to integrate the information from different systems. Without the ability to obtain detailed performance data on individual businesses and work processes, many of the design archetypes discussed in this chapter would not be feasible.

The definition of an organization's primary customer determines the basic configuration of the organization's structure.

- The most critical decision in designing any organization is deciding who the primary customer is. This decision determines the arrangement of unit groupings and relative spans of control.

- Five basic structural configurations are appropriate for different strategies:
  - Low price
  - Local value creation
  - Global standard of excellence
  - Dedicated service relationship
  - Expert knowledge

- *Definition:* Span of control represents the range of resources for which a manager is given decision rights and is held accountable for performance.

- Depending on the configuration, span of control of market-facing and operating-core managers is adjusted to favor either customer responsiveness or internal economies.

- Managers must ensure that the needs of constituents are satisfied. When important constituents are outside the normal value chain, separate functions are created to satisfy their interests.

- The quality of an organization's information system defines the design possibilities that can be considered.

- The financial control function is responsible for ensuring that adequate information exists inside the firm to support accountability.

## ACTION STEPS

FIGURE 3-12

### Lever 1: Unit Structure

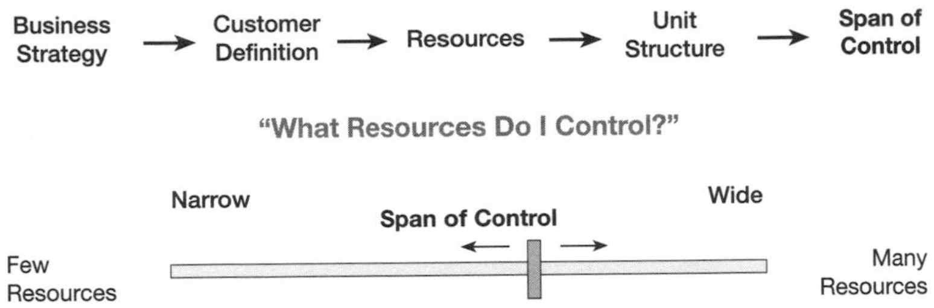

Business Strategy → Customer Definition → Resources → Unit Structure → Span of Control

**"What Resources Do I Control?"**

Narrow | Span of Control | Wide

Few Resources ←——————————————→ Many Resources

1. Using strategy as a guide, choose your primary customer from a list of constituents.

2. Determine which structural configuration best serves the needs of your primary customer.

3. Allocate balance sheet, production, and infrastructure resources to market-facing, operating-core, and constituent units.
   - Based on the desired level of customer responsiveness, adjust the span of control for market-facing units.
   - Based on the desired economies of scale and efficiencies, adjust the span of control for operating-core units.
   - Create dedicated units to meet the needs of important constituents.

4. Ensure that IT systems and financial controls are adequate to support the organization's structure and ensure its financial integrity.

# 4

---

# Diagnostic Control
# Systems

B UILDING AN ORGANIZATION from the ground up is like designing a building. In chapters 1 and 2, we laid the foundation.
In chapter 3, we erected the unit structure and dividers—the
floors and rooms that define working space. In this chapter, we
run the wiring—the accountability systems—that provides the
power to make everything work.

To better understand how to power up an organization, we
can refer to Ohm's Law, a basic formula in electronics:[1]

$$\text{Current} = \frac{\text{Voltage}}{\text{Resistance}}$$

Where

Current = Energy Flow (through a wire or circuit)

Voltage = Potential or Pressure

Resistance = Resistance to Energy Flow

In an organization, the left side of the formula—energy flow—is the value creation process. The right side of the equation shows that this energy can be increased in two ways: by increasing the pressure or potential in the system, or by decreasing the resistance. Potential in an organization is created by resources, and pressure comes from accountability to achieve results. Resistance, the denominator, represents human organizational barriers.

Thus, with some literary license we can rewrite this equation as follows:

$$\frac{\text{Value Creation in}}{\text{an Organization}} = \frac{\text{Potential} + \text{Pressure}}{\text{Resistance}}$$

$$= \frac{\text{Resources} + \text{Accountability}}{\text{Resistance}}$$

As this rewritten equation illustrates, designing an organization to create value requires attention to three sets of variables: resources, accountability (including incentives), and resistance. You tackled the first of these variables in chapter 3: how to configure resources, or span of control, for various strategic configurations. This chapter focuses on the remaining two variables: accountability and resistance.

## Choosing Performance Measures

When you construct a building, you must install a variety of wiring types for lighting, heating and cooling, appliances, and so on. The wires differ by size, color, and purpose. When you design an organization, you must also install a variety of performance measures.

Measures are always important for managers. As the chief technical officer of Microsoft stated, "To have scale you have to have accountability, and to have accountability you have to have numbers."[2] In any business, there are two types of measures: financial and nonfinancial. For financial measures, the unit of measurement is money: revenues, expenses, and profit. Nonfinancial measures are denominated in units other than money: quantities, reject rates, or market share.

To be effective, any measure—whether financial or nonfinancial—must meet three tests. First, a good measure must be *objective*: different people must be able to independently verify and agree upon its interpretation. The value of bank receipts recorded in a business's accounting system is an objective measure because different people reviewing the same information would calculate a consistent result. By contrast, the assessment of staff morale based on subjective interviews is not objective; different people may arrive at alternative conclusions.

Second, a good measure is *complete*: it captures all the relevant attributes of achievement. Daily profit tends to be a more complete measure of a bond trader's accomplishments than the number of sales calls made. Increasing the number of sales calls does not necessarily lead to more sales and profits.

Finally, a good measure is *responsive* to the efforts of the individual whose activities are being monitored. Thus, although share price may be responsive to the actions of a CEO, it is not a responsive measure of the accomplishments of a purchasing department manager.[3]

In addition to these basic technical attributes, good measures in any business should be clearly linked to economic value creation. Accounting measures can meet these tests if they are properly constructed from the three wheels of financial accountability (figure 4-1).[4] Accordingly, accounting measures are always important in a business.

To understand how to configure accounting measures to support organization design, let's start by looking at the center

**FIGURE 4-1**

## Three Wheels of Financial Accountability

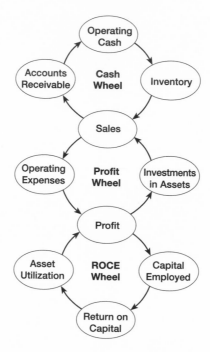

*Source:* R. Simons, "Templates for Profit Planning." HBS Note #199032. Reprinted by permission of the Harvard Business School.

wheel of figure 4-1: the profit wheel. This wheel represents four interdependent variables: sales, operating expenses, profit, and investment in assets. Some managers run market-facing units, with accountability for only one of these variables: sales revenue. These units are called *revenue centers*. Managers of revenue centers are typically measured on growth in volume and revenue, sometimes with additional targets for product mix and gross margin. It is clear what they are expected to maximize, and revenue center managers have relatively few tradeoffs to consider.

Other managers may be accountable for the second variable on the profit wheel: operating expenses. In this case, they are managers of *cost centers*—again, with relatively few tradeoffs.

Many operating-core units are managed as cost centers. Cost center managers are accountable for minimizing cost for a given level of output, or for maximizing output for a fixed level of costs.

*Profit center* managers are accountable for both revenues and costs. Instead of simply working to meet specific revenue or expense targets, they are expected to make tradeoffs between revenues and expenses to meet or exceed profit goals. The final variable on the profit wheel is investment in assets. Profits are the primary source of such investment, which in turn is used to fund future sales.

In addition to the variables on the profit wheel, financial accountability may include variables on the top wheel of figure 4-1—the cash wheel. Managing cash effectively is important in any business. Managers must ensure that goods and services sold on account have a high likelihood of collectability, accounts receivable must be turned into cash as quickly as possible, and inventory turnover—which supports sales and cost of goods sold—must be managed carefully to avoid excessive carrying costs.[5]

Kevin Rollins, vice chairman of Dell Computer, describes the importance of such measures in his company:

> At Dell, we use the balance sheet and the fundamentals of the P&L on a monthly basis as tools to manage operations. From the balance sheet, we track three cash-flow measures very closely. We look at weekly updates of how many days of inventory we have, broken out by product component. We can then work closely with our suppliers so we end up with the right inventory. When it's not quite right, we can use our direct-sales model to steer customers toward comparable products that we do have. So we use inventory information to work both the front and back ends at the same time.
>
> We also track and manage receivables and payables very tightly. This is basic blocking and tackling, but we give it a high priority. The payoff is that we have a negative cash-

conversion cycle of five days—that is, we get paid before we have to pay our suppliers. Since our competitors usually have to support their resellers by offering them credit, the direct model gives us an inherent cost advantage. And the more we can shorten our cash-collection cycle, the greater our advantage.[6]

In virtually all businesses, managers are accountable for revenue, expenses, and profit. Many firms add additional accountability for current assets using variables on the cash wheel. However, relatively few firms—only the best managed—expand accountability to the ROCE (return on capital employed) wheel to include the resources used to achieve profit.

Return on capital employed (sometimes called return on invested capital or return on net assets) is the ratio of net operating income divided by the assets employed in generating that profit.[7] For example, a business that earned $36 million profit using operating assets valued at $200 million would have an ROCE of 18 percent. To avoid distortion from out-of-date book values, some firms choose to value assets using replacement cost. Going one step further, some firms charge an interest cost for the assets used by the business unit. Then, instead of a simple ratio, the calculation yields what is called residual income or economic value added (EVA).

Although the intention here is not to offer a primer on ROCE calculations, the lesson is clear: unlike the profit wheel and cash wheel, where accounting systems provide relatively objective measures, ROCE calculations are subject to a number of design choices.[8]

Coming back to organization design, it is important to emphasize that the financial accountability system must be capable of collecting, aggregating, and distributing accounting data to support the chosen unit structure. For example, firms following a local value creation strategy must be able to track profit, cash flow, and capital employed in each region. Andy Taylor, CEO of Enterprise Rent-a-Car, describes the importance of generating such performance data at each one of its five thousand locations:

> We issue 5,000-plus financial statements a month. Our branch managers know exactly how well they did. They've got their customer satisfaction scores; they've got their bottom line. They can see right down to what it costs to wash each car. Enterprise is a confederation of these small businesses and we view ourselves here [at headquarters] as a switching station for the best ideas.[9]

This may seem an obvious point, but it is surprising how many companies are constrained in their organizing choices because of deficiencies in their accounting systems. In many cases, there is a mismatch between accounting data and the actual work performed by individual organizational units. For example, many accounting systems cannot calculate profit per customer, product, or project. In these cases, managers may find it impossible to adopt the dedicated service relationship configuration or the global standard of excellence configuration. Unfortunately, managers often choose unit structures that cannot be supported by their current accounting systems and hope for the best. This approach is doomed to failure: organization designs without commensurate accountability are, by definition, unworkable.

Of course, accounting measures tell only part of the story. In addition to accounting measures, managers typically are accountable for nonfinancial measures. These measures are needed to track both intangible resources (which accounting measures fail to capture) and strategically important initiatives.

# LEVER 2: DIAGNOSTIC CONTROL SYSTEMS

Like electrical wire on a spool, measures are of little use until installed and powered up. Measures are converted into systems of accountability when they are used as part of a diagnostic control system. This is the second lever of organization design (figure 4-2).

*Diagnostic control systems* are the formal information systems that managers use to monitor organizational outcomes and correct deviations from preset standards of performance.[10] Diagnostic control systems are used to set goals and monitor the performance of inanimate objects (an assembly machine), business groupings (departments or business units), and individual managers. Common diagnostic control systems include sales forecasting systems, budgets and profit plans, balanced scorecards, project milestone monitoring systems, and technology development systems.

**FIGURE 4-2**

**Lever 2: Diagnostic Control Systems**

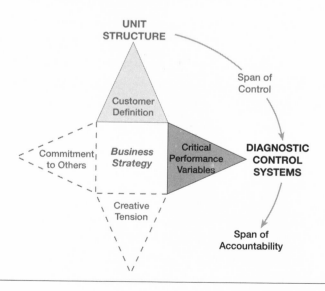

These systems are more than collections of measures. Diagnostic control systems measure the outputs of a process using a predetermined standard or goal as a benchmark. Managers use this variance information to correct deviations from standards.[11]

For purposes of organization design, four issues relating to diagnostic control systems are important:

- Identifying critical performance

- Determining span of accountability

- Powering up the system

- Overcoming resistance to measurement

## IDENTIFYING CRITICAL PERFORMANCE VARIABLES

Chapter 3 discussed the first of the four Cs: customer definition. Now we introduce the second C: critical performance variables. A *critical performance variable* is a factor that must be achieved or implemented for the intended strategy of the business to succeed.[12]

Since accounting measures are linked tightly to economic value creation, critical performance variables in any competitive business always include a subset of measures from the three wheels of financial accountability. But financial accounting numbers are rarely sufficient. Accounting measures typically do a poor job of communicating the details of a business strategy to the employees who are responsible for its implementation. Financial performance numbers are typically lagging indicators. They are an *outcome* of doing other things well—for example, building good products, launching effective marketing campaigns, creating customer loyalty. Moreover, a singular focus on financial measures can encourage people to make decisions that maximize short-term accounting returns at the expense of longer-term strategic investments.

Thus, to identify the appropriate critical performance variables, managers must analyze the factors that are responsible for success in implementing their strategy. These underlying performance variables are the keys to differentiating products and services from those of competitors and achieving value in the eyes of the customer.

The deductive analysis of critical performance variables has a long history reaching back almost fifty years. Such performance variables have variously been called critical success factors, key performance indicators, and, more recently, performance drivers. In the most recent innovation, Kaplan and Norton propose a technique of creating strategy maps to visually depict the flows of value creation inside a firm.[13] Starting with human resources and infrastructure, they argue, managers should sketch or map the sequential internal drivers of value creation, specifically those relating to key processes, customer responsiveness, and financial drivers of success.

Such a strategy map for an online bank is reproduced in figure 4-3.

The strategy story told in figure 4-3 is the following: an online service bank has three strategic objectives: (1) to add and retain high-value customers, (2) to increase revenue per customer, and (3) to reduce cost per customer. These goals are shown at the top of figure 4-3. To achieve these goals, managers begin by building a foundation or infrastructure that allows learning and growth. As shown at the bottom of the diagram, this foundation will be built by hiring key staff, planning for succession, achieving technical excellence, developing the company's culture, and using a balanced scorecard.

Moving up the chart, you can see that the next requirement relates to leveraging capabilities to create and sustain key internal processes: developing marketing programs, developing superior

FIGURE 4-3

## National Bank's Online Financial Service Strategy Map

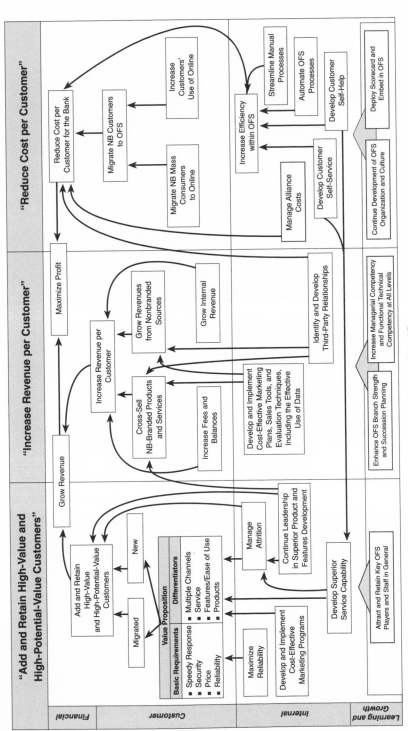

Source: From Kaplan and Norton, 2001: 110. Reprinted by permission of the Harvard Business School Press.

service capability, creating new products, developing third-party relationships, managing alliance costs, and automating and stream-lining internal processes.

These internal capabilities will, in turn, allow the bank to ef-fectively focus on the customer by developing a value proposi-tion, migrating and adding new customers, increasing fees and balances, cross-selling bank and nonbank products, and migrat-ing customers away from traditional bank channels to the new online services channels.

Finally, success with customers will—as shown at the top of the strategy map—lead to increased revenues, reduced costs, and maximum profits.

Thus, the boxes and arrows in the strategy map represent objectives that everyone in this business should focus on to im-plement the strategy and achieve the intended results. Each box represents a critical performance variable, and the arrows repre-sent the cause-and-effect relationships that managers believe underpin value creation.

After managers determine critical performance variables via the strategy mapping analysis, the final step is to define measures—financial and nonfinancial—for each variable, then group these measures into business, department, and personal scorecards.[14]

## INTRODUCING SPAN OF ACCOUNTABILITY

Chapter 3 introduced the concept of span of control—the as-signment of resources and decision rights to individual positions and units. Span of control defines the "what": the resources available to a specific manager to accomplish his or her job. But span of control does not give any insight into the specific goals that individual managers are expected to achieve—that is, how they are to achieve those goals.

We remedy this shortcoming by introducing the second of our four spans: *span of accountability*. This is defined as the range of tradeoffs that affects the performance measures used to evaluate a manager's achievements. Like span of control, span of accountability can fall along a continuum from wide to narrow.

The essential feature of span of accountability is the extent to which a manager is expected to make tradeoffs to achieve the desired levels of performance. With a narrow span of accountability, managers (e.g., cost or revenue center managers) are accountable only for a thin slice of organizational functioning and, as a result, have few tradeoffs available to achieve objectives related to their performance measures. For example, holding a procurement manager accountable for the cost of raw materials in a production line creates a narrow span of accountability. In this case, only a limited number of tradeoffs are available to affect the cost of raw materials—for example, changing suppliers, substituting inputs, and choosing different freight carriers.

By contrast, with a wide span of accountability, managers (e.g., profit center managers) are expected to consider a much wider range of tradeoffs to achieve their objectives. For example, a manager may be accountable for measures such as business profit, return on assets, or share price. With such measures, the range of variables and tradeoffs that affect the measure is wide. It includes almost anything inside and outside the firm that has the potential to affect current and future revenues and costs.

Consider a business manager who is accountable for return on capital employed. This manager has wide span of accountability, encompassing both net operating income and the level of assets used to generate those profits. But that span of accountability can be narrowed, as illustrated in the decomposition of ROCE using the DuPont formula:[15]

$$\text{ROCE} = \frac{\text{Net Income}}{\text{Capital Employed}} = \frac{\text{Net Income}}{\text{Sales}} \times \frac{\text{Sales}}{\text{Operating Assets}}$$

As this decomposition illustrates, ROCE accountability can be split between two managers: one manager can be held accountable only for profitability (net income ÷ sales), whereas the other manager is accountable for asset turnover (sales ÷ operating assets). Each manager is accountable only for a subset of ROCE, and, accordingly, each has a narrower span of accountability.

The narrowing of span of accountability is illustrated in figure 4-4. Moving from left to right, you can see that the broad ROCE measure can be broken into narrow measures that focus on individual financial accounts such as inventories and accounts receivable. Thus, span of accountability can be represented as a hierarchy from wide to narrow—either focusing on higher-level, broadly defined output measures (the left side of figure 4-4) or focusing on narrowly defined inputs and processes (the right side).

**FIGURE 4-4**

**ROCE and Span of Accountability**

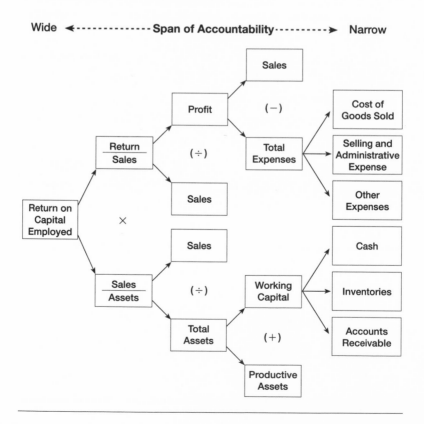

FIGURE 4-5

## Span of Accountability

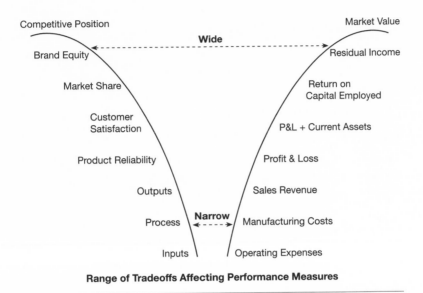

Range of Tradeoffs Affecting Performance Measures

Of course, organizations have many nonfinancial measures for inputs, processes, and outputs, and these measures also can be arrayed along a continuum of a wide to narrow span of accountability. For example, if a manager is accountable for a measure that represents a wide span of accountability, such as market share, he or she must consider multiple variables to attempt to influence the measure. By contrast, accountability for narrow input or process measures, such as headcount or material costs, will limit the tradeoffs available.

The hierarchy of span of accountability is illustrated in figure 4-5 for financial as well as nonfinancial measures.

## Decentralizing Decision Making

The statement that "authority should match responsibility" is one of the familiar tenets of organization design: the wider an individual's responsibility, the more authority he or she should have over the resources needed to accomplish the desired results. Thus, it is entirely appropriate for a purchasing manager to have a narrower span of accountability (e.g., cost of production inputs) than the CEO, who typically has both the widest span of accountability—encompassing business profit and stock price—and the widest span of control.

The extent of centralization or decentralization in decision making refers to the vertical distribution of span of accountability. As a rule, span of accountability widens as we move up an organization hierarchy, but the shape of this relationship may be quite different across organizations. In a highly centralized organization, senior managers alone have the right to make tradeoffs among critical financial and nonfinancial variables.

The span of accountability for a centralized organization is illustrated in the left panel of figure 4-6—a picture that looks like a pedestal sink. The span of accountability at the base of the organization is narrow, but it widens dramatically for the most senior managers.

By contrast, the right panel of figure 4-6 presents the span of accountability in a more decentralized organization; here, the diagram looks like a funnel. Decision making and the ability

**FIGURE 4-6**

## Span of Accountability and Decision Making

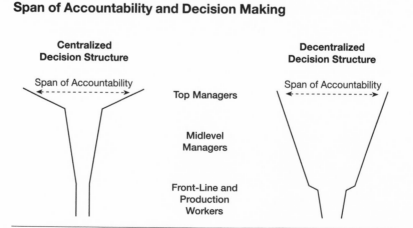

to make tradeoffs are pushed low; the span of accountability widens rapidly at relatively low levels.

## TURNING EMPLOYEES INTO ENTREPRENEURS

Let's now return to one of the fundamental tensions of organization design: the tension between accountability, on the one hand, and adaptability, on the other. Chapter 3 discussed how managers tilt resources to either market-facing or operating-core units to promote responsiveness or efficiency. But allocating resources does not, by itself, reconcile this tension.

If senior managers want flexibility and innovation in the work of a particular position, they must decentralize decision making and hold managers accountable for measures with a wide span of accountability. Subordinate managers can then consider tradeoffs and new initiatives in an attempt to influence the measure. If, on the other hand, senior managers desire standardization to drive efficiencies—an approach that may be appropriate for certain tasks—then they must hold subordinates accountable for measures with a narrow span of accountability. Key decisions are centralized, and few tradeoffs are allowed.

However, you cannot properly set the span of accountability to be either narrow or wide without reference to span of control. Consider a manager who finds herself accountable for measures that are much wider than her span of control. For example, a marketing manager may be held accountable for brand profit, but significant aspects of revenue and expenses (e.g., cost of goods sold, distribution costs, R&D) may depend on the actions of other people and groups over which she has no direct control. Similarly, a manager may be held accountable for customer loyalty, but the factors that affect loyalty—the initial purchase decision, after-sales service, advertising, depreciation in value over time—may be largely outside any one individual's control.

What happens when span of accountability is greater than span of control? An initial answer may be frustration. But more often than not, individuals must persist in finding ways of solving problems and capturing opportunities when they do not control all the resources that they need for success. They must step outside their span of control and enlist the aid and resources of others in the organization.

*Entrepreneurship* is defined as "the process by which individuals—either on their own or inside organizations—pursue opportunities without regard to the resources they currently control."[16] When managers set the span of accountability greater than the span of control, they force employees to become entrepreneurial. Thus, we can refer to the gap illustrated in figure 4-7 as the "entrepreneurial gap."

As mentioned earlier, one of the tenets of organization design is that span of accountability should be aligned with span of control; in other words, authority should match responsibility. When these two spans are aligned, managers are said to have *line of sight* in their performance measures: they control the resources needed to influence the measures for which they are accountable.

However, there is often a good reason for creating an entrepreneurial gap by setting span of accountability greater than

FIGURE 4-7

**Creating the Entrepreneurial Gap**

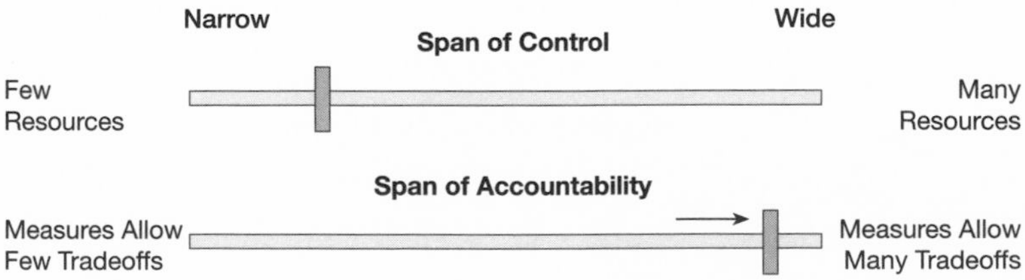

span of control. As customers become more educated and demanding and as markets become more competitive, innovation and flexibility become increasingly critical to success. Managers must drive flexibility and innovation deeper into their organizations. Accordingly, managers at relatively low levels are finding that they are being held accountable for measures with a wider span of accountability than ever before. To achieve what is asked of them, they must become entrepreneurs, drawing on their ingenuity, interpersonal networks, and influence skills to pull together the resources needed to achieve their goals.

Of course, such organizational pressure, if carried to an extreme, can be dysfunctional. Managers must exercise judgment to ensure that the gap between span of accountability and span of control is not so wide as to breed frustration or fear of failure. Also, to the extent that managers want to create an entrepreneurial gap, they must ensure that their employees have the personal qualities (e.g., initiative and resourcefulness) to be successful entrepreneurs within the existing organizational context.

## STANDARDIZING OPERATIONS

In many circumstances—typically when safety, quality, and adherence to standards are important concerns—managers may not want employees to be entrepreneurial. For example, managers of a nuclear power plant will not want plant operators to experiment or innovate with key reactor processes. Safety is too critical to tolerate mistakes.

You can probably think of many instances when senior managers will want to ensure standardization, specialization, and a focus on cost efficiencies and safety. To do so, they will narrow the span of accountability to reduce the range of tradeoffs embedded in the performance measurement system. Span of accountability will be set equal to, or sometimes even narrower

**FIGURE 4-8**

### Standardizing Operations

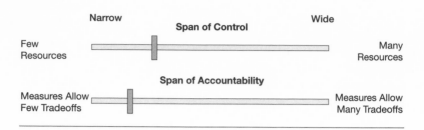

than, span of control. Decisions regarding tradeoffs will be reserved for senior managers (figure 4-8).

Consider a nuclear power plant manager overseeing complex thermal reactor processes. Decision rights are carefully constrained by standard operating procedures, and plant operators are allowed to make very few tradeoffs regarding operating parameters. Span of accountability is very narrow. Detailed performance metrics monitor compliance. In this case, span of accountability is significantly narrower than span of control.

Chapter 3 discussed how national low-price retailers such as Wal-Mart and TJX (operating discount stores Marshalls and T.J. Maxx) organize their stores by region. But store managers have narrow spans of control: they are precluded from changing signage, store layouts, hours of operation, displays, merchandise arrays, and so on. At Wal-Mart's thirty-five hundred stores, even temperature levels and lighting are controlled by computers in centralized operating-core units.[17] To ensure that procedures are implemented according to store policies, performance measures focus on specific operating variables and permit relatively few tradeoffs. Store managers are accountable for implementing standard operating procedures (carefully detailed in operating manuals), maximizing sales transactions, and controlling shrinkage (theft) and labor utilization. In other words, their span of accountability is narrow—sometimes even narrower than their span of control.[18]

The importance of standardization, specialization, and cost efficiencies is not limited to the low-price design. To standardize brand attributes, ensure operating safety, or otherwise ensure compliance with corporate standards, managers in any firm may limit tradeoffs by setting span of accountability narrower than span of control. Innovation and entrepreneurial activity are discouraged in favor of compliance.

Richard Hackman describes a similar approach in the operating procedures of modern aircraft. Studies of flight disasters by the Federal Aviation Administration often result in additional flight procedures and new cockpit management devices (e.g., a safety guard on a switch) designed to eliminate the possibility of pilot error. The effect is to tightly specify *how* the aircraft is flown, removing discretion from the hands of the pilot.

In this instance, commercial pilots have a relatively wide span of control (direct control and final decision rights regarding aircraft safety and operation), but their span of accountability is narrowed by performance measures that monitor compliance with government regulations and company operating procedures. However, Hackman cautions that a perverse consequence often results: with the use of more standard operating procedures and compliance monitoring, pilots are lulled into a false sense of security, and accordingly they pay less attention to flight details than they would if they were more personally accountable for choosing how to fly the aircraft in any given situation.[19] In other words, a focus on compliance drives out independent initiative.

Typically there is an inverse relationship between the number of measures and the span of accountability. The CEO of McDonald's has a wide span of accountability and yet may be accountable for only three measures: stock price, earnings per share, and competitive market position. By contrast, the manager of a McDonald's restaurant has a very narrow span of accountability and yet is accountable for compliance with many specific measures, standard operating procedures, rulebooks, and authorization levels.

We can generalize: when the intent is to standardize, a large number of input and process measures typically are used to monitor and ensure detailed compliance with management's directives. Degrees of freedom are reduced with each additional measure. Collectively, these input and process measures allow little in terms of tradeoffs and discretion, reflecting a narrow span of accountability. Thus, we could redraw figure 4-5 to include not only the span of accountability—from narrow to wide—but also the number of measures associated with the relative spans of accountability: the wider the span, the fewer the number of measures (figure 4-9).

**FIGURE 4-9**

## Relationship Between Number of Measures and Span of Accountability

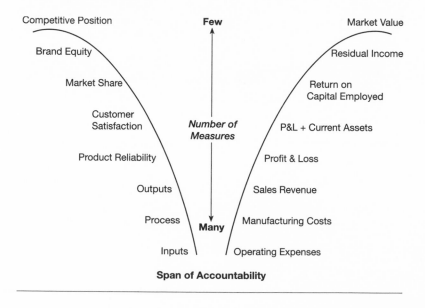

# ADJUSTING SPAN OF ACCOUNTABILITY TO IMPLEMENT STRATEGY

After choosing the basic structure and configuration of an organization, managers must make decisions about the span of accountability for *each* operating-core and market-facing unit. This is one of the most important decisions in creating organizations to implement strategy effectively.

Managers of market-facing units for which customer responsiveness is paramount (e.g., in a local value creation design) typically operate with wide spans of accountability to ensure flexibility, innovation, and customer responsiveness. Creative tradeoffs will be encouraged. According to the span of accountability menu presented in figure 4-9, these managers—and the teams they lead—may be accountable for a small number of broad measures. On the financial side, these measures include profit or return on capital employed; on the nonfinancial side, they include customer satisfaction or market share. Equally important from a design perspective, their span of accountability will likely exceed their span of control. The intention of senior managers is to stimulate entrepreneurial behavior as they attempt to create value for customers and differentiate products and services in the marketplace.

The design sliders of figure 4-10 present this choice graphically. Span of control is wide, but span of accountability is even wider.

**FIGURE 4-10**

## Market-Facing Unit—Local Value Creation Design

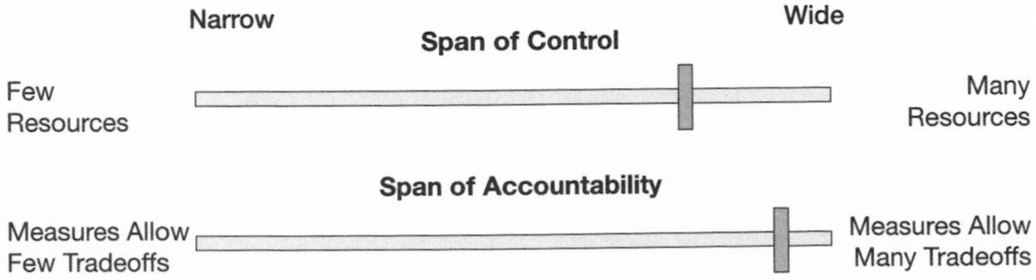

FIGURE 4-11

## Market-Facing Unit—Low-Price Design

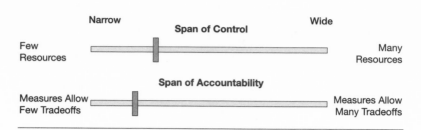

For a low-price configuration such as a fast food franchise, the design sliders for the market-facing units would be set very differently, as illustrated in figure 4-11. Span of control is narrow, and span of accountability is narrower still. The intention is to ensure compliance with brand standards. In this design, store operators are accountable for many detailed input and process measures that limit choice and discretion.

For operating-core units, where efficiency and economies of scale are paramount, managers will be given relatively large spans of control. They will have large-scale resources, but their span of accountability will be relatively narrow. For these units, flexibility and innovation are less important than efficiency and cost minimization. Work can, and should, be standardized. On the financial accountability wheels, measures include specific line item operating expenses; nonfinancial measures include narrowly defined levels of inputs, processes, and outputs. This choice is illustrated with the design sliders in figure 4-12.

## POWERING UP THE SYSTEM

After the wiring is completed in an electrical system, a switch must be thrown to connect the system to a power supply. The switch that delivers power in organizations is incentives. Indi-

**FIGURE 4-12**

**Operating-Core Unit—Low-Price Design**

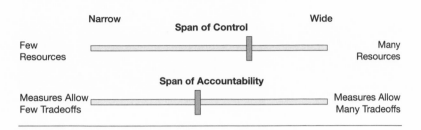

viduals must be rewarded for achievements on the measures for which they are accountable. Of course, incentives can include more than purely financial rewards. People often derive important intrinsic rewards from recognition, personal achievement, and teamwork. Chapter 6 will pursue the implications and power of such intrinsic rewards.

In businesses, financial incentives are generally used to power up diagnostic control systems. Incentives can be either hardwired or softwired. A *hardwired incentive* represents a direct connection between goals, results, and rewards. Payouts are determined by a preset formula. Generally, it seems that hardwired incentives would be a preferred option because they provide goal clarity and objectivity in the application of measures and rewards. Unfortunately, hardwired reward systems are notoriously problematic for three reasons. First, to increase the likelihood of receiving rewards, people may attempt to negotiate lower goals. As Rosabeth Kanter has stated, "One of the great innovation-killers is the admonition 'You must deliver on your promises.' What happens? To avoid failure, people promise only the most limited goals."[20]

Second, after the formula is set, individuals may attempt to game the system by taking actions that maximize the payout formula but do not lead to desired results. This problem can arise when a measure is responsive to an individual's actions but incomplete as a measure of value creation. For example, if salespeople are paid on the number of units of a particular product shipped, they may try to induce customers to accept that product even if it is not the best one for their needs. In addition, people may be induced to hide bad news that could negatively impact their bonus. Worse, some people may distort data by manipulating accounting entries or falsifying records to ensure that they receive the rewards they desire.

Finally, with preset goals and rewards, there is often little incentive for workers to go the extra mile after they earn the full bonus, or to take on tasks that are not explicitly rewarded as part of the payout formula. In discussing pay for performance, Brickley, Smith, and Zimmerman remind us, "You get what you pay for—and frequently, that is all you get."[21]

For these reasons, managers may choose *softwired incentives*, which are determined subjectively based on effort. This approach has the advantage of giving managers flexibility in recognizing innovation, entrepreneurship, and unique contributions in support of the implementation of strategy. If contribution is rewarded subjectively, subordinates will be motivated to communicate changing conditions and showcase the actions that they are taking to respond. For a softwired reward system to be effective, however, two conditions are necessary. First, subordinates must trust the ability of their superiors to accurately and fairly calibrate contribution. And, second, superiors must be willing to invest a significant amount of time and attention to truly understand what is happening in the business and to fairly calibrate the efforts and skills of subordinates in changing circumstances.[22]

Given the amount of management attention required to make subjective rewards effective, managers generally prefer to use hardwired incentives. However, because of the risks, managers should use hardwired incentives only when internal control systems are adequate to minimize gaming.

## OVERCOMING RESISTANCE TO MEASUREMENT

Recall the equation at the beginning of this chapter: Value creation is equal to resources plus accountability, divided by resistance. We have discussed resources and accountability at length. However, to achieve maximum energy in any organization, managers must find a way to counter the human resistance that is an inherent part of any measurement process.

As with a faulty electrical system, there are a variety of reasons individuals resist or fail to respond to diagnostic control systems. These factors can be broken into five causes:

- Confusing goals

- Conflicting incentives

- Misalignment of accountability and control

- Faulty connection to value creation

- Inadequate competence and skills

### Confusing Goals

It may seem too obvious to state, but people become confused when accountability measures conflict with an organization's strategy. For example, top managers of a global bank wanted to change their strategy to focus on large corporate customers that operated in multiple regions of the world. Even though senior managers announced their new strategy with great fanfare, they did not change their measures, continuing to focus primarily on revenue and profit by country. The gap between strategic intent and accountability made it virtually impossible to successfully implement the new strategy.

The process of creating measures and targets—drawing strategy maps and balanced scorecards—is intended to overcome this type of resistance. As the saying goes, what gets measured gets managed.

Unfortunately, sometimes well-intentioned techniques for clarifying goals and objectives can serve instead to muddy the waters. This can be true, for example, when individuals feel overwhelmed by the number of measures for which they are accountable. It is common for organizations to create balanced scorecards with thirty, forty, fifty, or more measures. In an electrical system, the amount of energy is finite: every wire and circuit added to the system creates additional resistance and absorbs more energy. The same is true in organizations: attention is limited. Having too many measures dilutes energy and obscures priorities. It becomes hard to know what to focus on. An excessive number of measures causes confusion about desired goals.

Elsewhere, I have written that a good rule of thumb in accountability systems is to ensure that individuals are accountable for no more measures than they can remember—usually about seven.[23] This is based on a famous article titled "The Magic Number Seven: Plus or Minus Two," by psychologist G. Miller. In his analysis, Miller argues that individuals become overwhelmed if they must process too many bits of information. Conversely, if there are too few bits of information, there is not enough variety to stimulate creativity.

Business scorecards may attempt to replicate a systems dynamics model with tens, if not hundreds, of measures, but managers should carefully restrict the number of measures for individual accountability. They must take care not to overload the circuits—in this case, the cognitive processing capabilities of human beings.

So an important—but often neglected—step in identifying critical performance variables and in building scorecards is to assign accountability for the measures to individual managers. It is not enough to create a strategy map and business scorecard. If you present managers with scorecards containing up to forty or fifty measures without clear individual accountability, resistance is inevitable.

## Conflicting Incentives

A well-known article in the organizational literature is titled "On the Folly of Rewarding A While Hoping for B."[24] This title aptly captures a pervasive organizational problem: often, people are rewarded for behaviors that are different from the behavior that senior managers say they desire.

This short circuit between goals and rewards is most frequently encountered in the tension between financial and nonfinancial results. Often, a manager is accountable for scorecard measures that include both financial and nonfinancial measures. Notwithstanding a desire to "balance" the scorecard, managers may tie bonuses disproportionately to financial measures. This is especially true when individuals perform well on nonfinancial measures but poorly on financial measures. In these cases, the weight of bonus payouts is usually skewed heavily to the financial measures. As a result, nonfinancial measures will have little impact on behavior. And actions always speak louder than words. People throughout the organization will quickly learn what is rewarded, and they will respond accordingly.

## Misalignment of Accountability and Control

Using an incorrectly sized wire can cause failure in an electrical system. Similarly, managers must choose the right span of accountability for the task they desire to accomplish.

As discussed earlier, managers must adjust span of accountability to get the right balance between innovation and standardization. But this is sometimes a complicated task. Moving the slider toward broad measures with wide spans of accountability can result in frustration when resources are not available to make the necessary tradeoffs. Although you may want your subordinates to exercise their creative capacity to do more with less, there comes a point where subordinates may give up because they perceive the task to be unreasonably difficult. In such cases, energy will be lost to grumbling, gaming, and a sense of frustration.

Similarly, moving the slider too far toward detailed measures with a narrow span of accountability can choke off innovation. Lately, there has been a great deal of enthusiasm for balanced scorecards and other new performance measurement systems. The benefits of these systems flow from the ability they give managers to articulate and communicate strategy to everyone in the organization—and hold individuals accountable for implementation according to scorecard measures.

Often, however, scorecard designers identify drivers, measures, and accountabilities without regard for the span of control of the individuals accountable for the measures. Thus, they may unwittingly create inappropriate gaps between span of control and span of accountability.

Consider what happens when multiple input and process measures effectively limit the tradeoffs that managers are allowed to consider. For example, instead of holding a subordinate manager accountable for profit (a single broad measure), you might narrow the span of accountability by setting separate targets for revenue and operating expenses. As a result, when the opportunity arises to take on new business, the manager may be forced to forego the incremental profit because of anticipated increases in operating expenses. The creation of narrow measures—essentially telling the manager *how* he or she is expected to make tradeoffs between revenue and expense to implement strategy—has reduced individual flexibility.

This approach is similar to the "scientific management" championed by Fredrick Taylor a century ago.[25] Scientific management rested on four principles: (1) gathering objective data to allow management to record, classify, and reduce tasks to scientific rules; (2) selecting workers fitted for these specific tasks; (3) training workers to do their job in accordance with these rules; and (4) providing piece-rate incentives for outputs. Staff experts analyzed tasks and created detailed process guidelines and measures to ensure compliance. The result was to limit tradeoffs in the name of increased efficiency.

Today, the focus is often the same: the creation of input and process measures that can be monitored by superiors. Work is broken down and parceled out to individual managers, and their compliance—as measured by a performance scorecard—is tracked and rewarded.

But as workers become more educated and entrepreneurial, they sometimes resist having their work measured and monitored by detailed input and process measures. This risk is acute when scorecard designers—often staff specialists or consultants—think that they know best how individuals throughout the organization should create value. People may resist by sabotaging the measurement system or by simply disregarding the measures in the hope of discrediting the system.

Managers at 3M are sensitive to this problem. The senior vice president of research and development states, "Managers at 3M do perform such traditional tasks as clarifying the company's goals and setting objectives. We let our people know what we want them to accomplish. But—and it is a very big *but*—we do *not* tell them how to achieve those goals. We think that by giving employees the freedom to find new paths to new solutions, we are unleashing creativity."[26]

### Faulty Connection to Value Creation

If there is a short in the electrical system—an open circuit—energy will not reach its intended target. The system will be dead, and the light will not turn on or the furnace will not start. The same thing can happen in accountability systems.

As the sample strategy map in figure 4-3 illustrates, measures are embedded in a linked system of cause-and-effect variables. Strategy is a hypothesis. And, like any hypothesis, data may prove the strategy linkages to be false.

What happens if there is a short circuit in the strategy map? One of the benefits of strategy mapping is that it lets you perform an after-the-fact evaluation of the strategy linkages. After performance data is collected, the analysts who built the strategy map can analyze the results to verify that the strategy linkages are correctly specified. If outcome measures fail to respond to improvements in driver measures, then there is a bad connection—a false hypothesis—in the system. Managers and analysts can use the data to test the strategy map's validity.

However, experience with post-audits in capital budgeting systems is not encouraging. Rarely does anyone take the time to go back to check the validity of early calculations and projections. Circumstances change, consultants are no longer engaged, and the people responsible for the implementation of the scorecard have moved on to new responsibilities. Moreover, managers deep in the organization often do not need to wait for ex post data to confirm their hypotheses. They already know, based on personal experience and an intimate understanding of customers and markets, what does and doesn't create value.

### Inadequate Competence and Skills

The discussion so far has taken the skills and competence of people as given—and sufficient for the task. But, of course, it is easy to imagine situations when individuals do not have the requisite aptitude and skills: not everyone can respond creatively and productively when given a wide span of accountability, demanding goals, and insufficient resources. Training, expertise, and aptitude may fall short.

This risk was illustrated in the failed implementation of a new strategy by the Store24 convenience chain. In an attempt to increase market share, senior management decided to move away from its traditional "speed and efficiency" strategy by creating a fun and entertaining shopping environment. The new strategy was called "Ban Boredom." Managers were measured, evaluated, and rewarded on their ability to create promotions that would entertain customers by, for example, placing life-size cutouts of movie stars in their stores. The new strategy failed, however, because of inconsistency in the skills of store managers: stores with more-skilled staff were able to improve sales and financial performance, suggesting that the new strategy was valid; but many stores were managed by individuals who did not have the requisite skills.[27] Frustration and poor outcomes were the inevitable result.

No electrical system can do more than it was designed to do; similarly, people must be matched to the right jobs. Different people have different abilities to be creative (or to work in settings where repetitive, standardized work is essential). Thus, it is no accident that firms such as General Electric devote more than $1 billion annually to executive training at their Leadership Center in Crotonville, New York. Such programs serve to enhance individual skills and help build personal networks that can support complex strategies (the subject of chapter 5).

## Ensuring Adequate Controls

The lack of accounting systems that are transparent, reliable, and consistent has doomed more than one well-crafted attempt to implement a strategy. If managers want to evaluate subordinates on measures such as global product profitability or ROCE, an information system must exist to calculate such metrics. Chapter 3 described Microsoft's change to a global standard of excellence configuration. Based on the discussion in this chapter, it should come as no surprise that one of the critical first steps in Microsoft's transition was to upgrade its diagnostic control systems: an "Executive P&L"—a new system capable of providing balance sheets, financial analysis, and performance measurement tools—was installed to allow managers of newly formed business units to understand their cost structures.[28]

Few of the techniques described in this chapter would be possible in large, global companies without sophisticated information technology infrastructures. Technology has allowed companies to centralize information and thereby increase accountability, push down decision rights to empower front-line workers, increase productivity through more efficient information exchange, and outsource significant operating-core functions. New capabilities based on Internet and wireless access continue to enlarge information capabilities in unpredictable ways.[29]

With this increase in capability, however, comes the need for caution. Never before has the technology of measurement been so powerful. The risk—alluded to earlier in this chapter—is that managers will measure too many variables and will hold subordinates accountable for the wrong things. Focus on the *critical* performance variables is lost as the ease of measurement increases and the cost of measurement declines. But measurement is always costly—in the opportunity cost of diverted attention.

Thus, managers and system designers must remain vigilant to ensure that the power of technology is not allowed to create confusion but instead is harnessed to increase efficiency and effectiveness.

In addition, managers must anticipate and control dangers that arise from the performance pressures created by the tech-

**FIGURE 4-13**

**A Dangerous Triad**

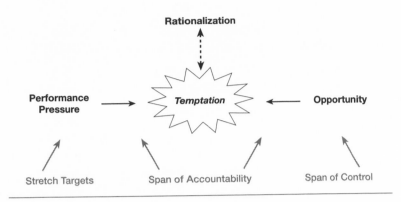

niques discussed in this chapter. The confluence of performance pressure, the opportunity to manipulate information or assets, and rationalization creates the dangerous triad illustrated in figure 4-13.[30]

*Performance pressure* arises from the measures, targets, and incentives created by diagnostic control systems. *Opportunity* arises from access to resources and the ability to cut corners or use assets improperly. Taken together, pressure and opportunity create *temptation* for individuals to lower quality standards or misstate revenue to achieve important targets and incentives. Most people in an organization will not succumb to such temptation unless one final ingredient is present: *rationalization*. If individuals can convince themselves that their contemplated behavior is not wrong—using excuses such as "Everybody does it," "The effect is immaterial," "No one is hurt," or "I'm doing it for the good of the company"—then there is little to prevent behaviors that might put both the individual and the business at risk.

To defuse the dangerous triad, managers must eliminate one of the three ingredients: pressure, opportunity, or rationalization. But as discussed in this chapter, performance pressure is often necessary to stimulate creativity and innovation. So, in general, managers must either eliminate the ability of people to rationalize unethical behavior or eliminate their opportunity to engage in unsound business practices. Strong levers of control are essential: clear boundaries must be communicated and enforced so that there is no ambiguity about the types of unethical and illegal behavior that will not be tolerated; sanctions, including dismissal, must be consistently enforced; strong internal controls (e.g., checks and balances such as segregation of duties, defined authorization levels, rotation in key jobs) must be installed and monitored by corporate accounting staff and internal auditors.[31]

The financial control organization—operating under titles such as finance, accounting and control, or the controller's department—is responsible for this important task. Its assignment is not only to design and maintain diagnostic control systems but also to ensure transparency, consistency, and compliance with ethical standards and codes of business conduct. These financial control functions are the bedrock of diagnostic control systems.

## CHAPTER THEME

The gap between span of accountability and span of control shapes entrepreneurial behavior.

## KEY CHAPTER IDEAS

- If you can't measure it, you can't manage it.

- *Definition:* A critical performance variable is a factor that must be achieved or implemented successfully for the intended strategy of the business to succeed. Critical performance variables for any business reflect both financial and nonfinancial measures.

- The financial accountability system must be capable of collecting, aggregating, and distributing accounting data to support the chosen unit structure. The ability to generate accounting data from the profit wheel, cash wheel, and ROCE wheel is a fundamental building block of organization design.

- *Definition:* Span of accountability is the range of tradeoffs affecting the performance measures used to evaluate a manager's achievements. Span of accountability can be wide or narrow.

- By setting span of accountability greater than span of control, senior managers can create pressure for individuals to become entrepreneurs. Alternatively, if managers wish to promote standardization and compliance, they can set span of accountability narrower than span of control.

- Resistance will occur if any of the following situations exist:
  - Goals are confusing because there are too many measures or the measures are misaligned with strategy.
  - Incentives are not aligned with goals and measures.
  - Span of control and accountability are misaligned.
  - Scorecard measures are not tested to ensure that they are valid.
  - Individuals lack necessary training and skills.

- The confluence of performance pressure, opportunity, and rationalization can create temptation for people to make bad, and sometimes unethical, decisions.

## ACTION STEPS

**FIGURE 4-14**

### Lever 2: Diagnostic Control Systems

Business Strategy → Critical Performance Variables → Measures and Rewards → Diagnostic Control Systems → Span of Accountability

**"What Performance Measures Am I Accountable For?"**

|  Narrow | | Wide |
|---|---|---|
| | **Span of Accountability** | |
| Measures Allow Few Tradeoffs | ← ∣ → | Measures Allow Many Tradeoffs |

1. Determine your organization's critical *financial* performance variables from the profit wheel, the cash wheel, and the ROCE wheel.

2. Determine the critical *nonfinancial* performance variables that reflect your strategy.

3. Create diagnostic control systems to communicate your goals and to monitor performance for all critical performance variables.

4. Based on your strategy and desired level of tradeoffs, design the span of accountability for all units and key management positions.

5. To ensure appropriate levels of innovation or standardization, adjust span of accountability relative to span of control.

6. Set your targets and align subordinates' incentives with your diagnostic control system measures.

7. Anticipate potential sources of resistance, and adjust your goals, targets, spans of accountability, and incentives accordingly.

# 5

---

# INTERACTIVE NETWORKS

CHAPTERS 3 AND 4 described how managers design organizations in much the same way that an architect designs a building. Starting with an understanding of intended purpose, the architect conceptualizes the overall structure and designs the dimensions of individual rooms. Then electrical systems are added to support the energy needs of the building and its occupants. As a final check, the architect considers anticipated traffic patterns to ensure that the building will facilitate the flow of people through rooms and between floors.

We have followed the same sequence. In chapters 1 and 2, we started with an organization's purpose and strategy. In chapter 3, we discussed how managers decide on the structure of work units. In chapter 4, we installed energy and monitoring systems through diagnostic controls and incentives.

Now it's time to look at the traffic flows. Does the structure facilitate or impede human interaction? How are information and new ideas transmitted and shared? Is the level of creativity appropriate to the strategy that managers are attempting to implement?

To answer these questions, we introduce interactive networks as the third lever of organization design. These networks,
which stimulate informal influence patterns, reconcile the tension between the ladders and rings discussed in chapter 1. Some
economists believe that *influence costs*—resources that individuals
devote to influencing organizational decisions to their benefit or
the benefit of their units—are detrimental to effective organizational functioning.[1] I argue the opposite: exerting influence is
not only healthy, but it is also essential for any organization in
which leaders want to stimulate innovation and adaptation.

## CREATIVE TENSION

Previous chapters analyzed customer definition and critical performance variables as two key determinants of organization
structure and systems. We now turn to the third of the four Cs:
*creative tension*. As with the other Cs, managers must first analyze
their strategy to determine the level of creative tension that they
desire. Then they must design the third lever—interactive networks—to facilitate the required levels of interunit communication, learning, and adaptation (figure 5-1).

One of the main purposes of organization design is to narrow people's focus and attention. Without such discipline, it
would be impossible to implement strategy in any large, complex organization. As Theodore Levitt noted, "Organizations
are created to achieve order. They have policies, procedures,
and formal or powerfully informal (unspoken) rules. The job
for which the organization exists could not possibly get done
without these rules, procedures, and policies. . . . Creativity and
innovation disturb order. Hence, organization tends to be in-
hospitable to creativity and innovation, though without creativity and innovation it would eventually perish."[2]

Given this inevitable inertia, a critical task of leadership is to
counterbalance the natural forces of stability that are embedded

FIGURE 5-1

## Lever 3: Interactive Networks

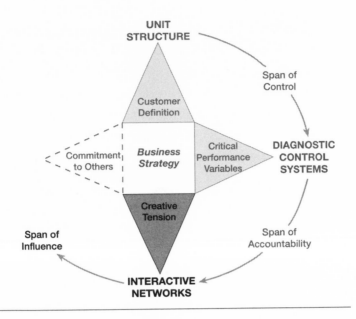

in any organization. Senior managers must stimulate the organization to constantly create and test new ideas. They must ensure that existing assumptions are challenged. Individuals at all levels must be forced to interact with people in other units and to focus on aspects of the business that are orthogonal (i.e., at right angles) to their current positions and job responsibilities. Over time, these interactions can sometimes lead to novel experiments and unexpected new strategies.

In popular parlance, people must think outside the box. But the organization designs described earlier have focused precisely on building the boxes from which managers may now want to escape.

I must, therefore, now acknowledge a critical shortcoming of the structural designs discussed in previous chapters. These structures and systems are intended to implement *current* strategy; they fail to take into account how an organization should evolve and adapt for the *future*. For an organization to remain vibrant over time, there must be constant pressure for people to innovate, think differently, and try new approaches to old problems. Without new ideas, organizations will become stuck in the past, and competitors will sooner or later overtake them.

Because of their insulating effect, the vertical ladders of accountability described in earlier chapters are often referred to pejoratively as silos, chimneys, or stovepipes. Yet, to allow organizations to adapt and learn, successful designs must encourage managers to interact across these silos. Managers of operating-core units must interact with units that are close to markets and customers; similarly, managers of market-facing units must be encouraged to interact with operating-core managers to learn how to enhance efficiencies, economies, and best operating practices. From these interactions, problems will be discussed, best practices shared, and new ideas generated.

To illustrate this point, let's revisit the local value creation configuration. This design—adopted by some automobile manufacturers, consumer product companies, and accounting firms—creates relatively independent business units in each separate geographic market to enhance responsiveness to local customer needs. But like any design, this choice involves tradeoffs. In this case, managers must accept higher costs that arise from the duplication of operating-core functions in each business unit. Managers who choose this design are willing to pay this price because the value of enhanced customer responsiveness is greater than the cost of lost efficiencies.

But managers of local value creation firms must still ensure that their firms do not fall too far behind competitors in implementing new technologies, cost efficiencies, and best practices. Without improvement in such areas—even though they are peripheral to the core strategy—products may become too expensive or technically obsolete in the marketplace. Without continuous improvement, the value proposition will inevitably erode and become less compelling to customers.

Similarly, in firms adopting a low-price configuration—big box retailers, low-expense mutual funds, discount-fare airlines—wide spans of control and accountability tilt power to large and efficient operating-core functions. Nevertheless, managers must still ensure that the firm does not lose focus on the dynamics of its competitive markets and the changing needs of its customers. Even with low prices, if managers fail to adapt their value proposition to changing market conditions, their firms will lose touch with customers, technology, and competition. Managers must find ways to ensure that employees who focus on operating efficiencies in their day-to-day jobs are still concerned about adapting the business to reflect changes in market dynamics.

One way to solve this problem is through job rotation programs, which force individuals to stand in the shoes of others—for a day, a week, or for six months. This can be an effective technique to build awareness of the issues faced by employees in different units as they attempt to meet customer needs or increase operating efficiencies. However, when senior managers decide that sustained levels of creative tension are needed throughout an organization, they must employ more broadly based and systematic approaches.

## SPAN OF INFLUENCE

To build the rings that will allow learning and adaptation, we now introduce the third span in our organization design model: span of influence. *Span of influence* defines the width of the net that an individual casts in collecting data, probing for new information, and attempting to influence the work of others. Consistent with the other spans in this analysis, span of influence is

**FIGURE 5-2**

**Narrow Span of Influence**

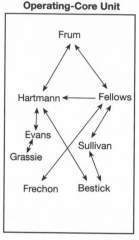

Operating-Core Unit

Unit
Boundary

defined primarily at the level of the individual and can fall any-where on a continuum from narrow to wide. Span of influence answers the question, "Who do I need to influence to achieve the goals for which I'm accountable?"

For some individuals, work is relatively self-contained. As a result, it is not necessary to interact with others outside their own units to accomplish their goals. In such situations, span of influence can be quite narrow. Figure 5-2 illustrates an operating-core unit where managers have relatively narrow spans of influence.

In many instances, however, a much wider span of influence is necessary. With interdependent tasks, individuals must figure out ways to navigate complex organizational pathways to achieve their goals.[3] They must cast a wide net both horizontally and vertically—collecting data, probing for new information, and at-tempting to influence the work of other people inside and out-side their own group. Figure 5-3 illustrates a unit where spans of influence are much wider.

**FIGURE 5-3**

## Wide Span of Influence

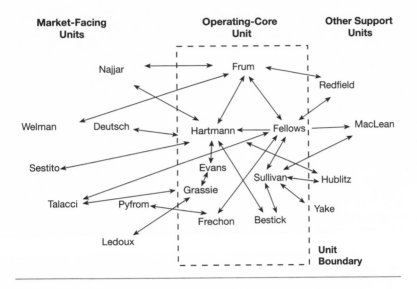

As an organization design variable, span of influence can—and must—be crafted as carefully as span of control and span of accountability. Based on specific strategies, customer needs, and product technologies, senior managers can choose to widen or narrow spans of influence for the various operating-core and market-facing units in their firm. If managers want high levels of creative tension to stimulate learning and adaptation, they will widen spans of influence so that members of market-facing and operating-core units are interacting regularly. To force people out of their silos, senior managers may adjust span of influence to be greater than span of control. Conversely, if managers want to ensure that employees are not distracted from their narrowly defined jobs, they will set span of influence narrowly.

At the individual level, a wide span of influence is often the manifestation of organizational power. As the CEO of consumer products company Procter & Gamble acknowledged, "The

**FIGURE 5-4**

### Marketing and Sales Unit—Wide Span of Influence

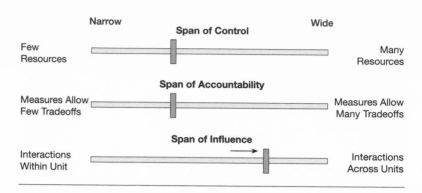

measure of a powerful person is that their circle of influence is greater than their circle of control."[4]

In figure 5-4, span of influence is set relatively wide in a marketing and sales unit where span of control and span of accountability are both relatively narrow. In this instance, unit managers neither control a broad range of resources nor have responsibility for a wide range of tradeoffs in their performance measures. Nevertheless, senior managers have widened span of influence for their marketing and sales managers to spark new ideas and stimulate the sharing of best practices across units.

## LEVER 3: INTERACTIVE NETWORKS

Managers inject creative tension into an organization—thereby forcing individuals to widen their peripheral vision and think in new and creative ways—by building interactive networks. *Interactive networks* are the structures and systems that stimulate individuals to gather information and to influence the decisions of others.

We have already discussed one of the principal mechanisms for designing such tension: creating an entrepreneurial gap by setting span of accountability greater than span of control. In addition to this technique for sparking creative tension, managers can create *dual influence structures* by overlaying a supplemental accountability structure on the organization design to bring people from different units together in newly formed work groups. They can also use *accounting and control systems* to create pressure for people to interact with those in other units who are striving to achieve different goals.

Of course, attempting to build interactive networks will be ineffective unless people in other units are willing to respond to requests for help. In chapter 6, therefore, I introduce the final span—span of support—as the necessary reciprocal to ensure that people throughout the organization are receptive to the interactive systems and structures that are the focus of this chapter.

## Building Dual Influence Structures

To increase creative tension, widen span of influence, and force individuals to think out of the box, managers can modify accountability in two ways:

- Adding an overlay of supplemental activities

- Adding a second boss

### Adding an Overlay of Supplemental Activities

To build temporary interactive networks, managers often form ad hoc task teams that cut across organizational boundaries. Task force initiatives might, for example, relate to developing quality improvement programs, enhancing speed to market, or finding ways for regions to work together more effectively.

Consider a task team formed to find ways of reducing costs by combining the purchasing power of multiple business units. Team members are drawn from the management ranks of market-facing units and from key operating-core functions. Before the team is formed, these individuals have not had the opportunity to interact and many do not know each other.

A senior vice president at General Electric explains how the company uses this technique:

> Horizontal turf boundaries . . . impede communication and slow response time . . . . GE aims to be a company without boundaries. In practice, that means we are continually organizing cross-functional innovation teams that include representatives from research, marketing, manufacturing, engineering, and service, as well as vendors and customers. . . . We are most effective if we have our team members sitting around one coffee pot, even if that requires spending a few months in a Wisconsin motel in the dead of winter. . . . In [some] cases, however, the requisite groups are scattered around the globe: the people responsible for overall design are in Great Britain; manufacturing is scheduled in Hungary; and the group that would develop the electronic ballast is in Ohio. The team members work together, bridging the physical distances with regular phone calls, e-mail, videoconferences, and extended visits in one or another of the project locations.[5]

Similar techniques are used in the U.S. Marine Corps. Super squadron task forces are routinely deployed around the world for assignments lasting up to a year. The mandate of each super squadron—made up of pilots from different individual squadrons—is to absorb and share best practices in each location the members visit. After the assignment is completed, each pilot returns to his original unit with new ideas and experiences to make his home squadron better.[6]

Because the work of task force teams bypasses traditional reporting relationships, a senior manager of sufficient stature is

FIGURE 5-5

## Dual Influence Structures

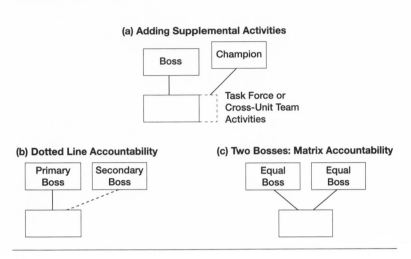

**(a) Adding Supplemental Activities**

Boss

Champion

Task Force or
Cross-Unit Team
Activities

**(b) Dotted Line Accountability**

Primary
Boss

Secondary
Boss

**(c) Two Bosses: Matrix Accountability**

Equal
Boss

Equal
Boss

usually asked to act as "champion" to give the group legitimacy and to create the impetus for team efforts. The champion—who typically is not the team members' day-to-day boss—assumes responsibility for guiding the work of the team and uses the power of his or her position to signal the importance of the cross-unit task (figure 5-5a).

Although the potential benefits of cross-unit interaction are high, the ability of ad hoc task teams to sustain energy is constrained. Not only is their time together limited by design, the implementation of team recommendations often involves resource commitments by many units and groups throughout the organization. Consequently, it is difficult (if not impossible) to measure and aggregate the overall benefits and costs of implementing the team's recommendations. Also, to the extent that the team produces recommendations for early-stage innovation, it is inherently difficult to assess the value of a potential implementation.

Because organizations usually do not have performance measurement systems that can evaluate the success of ad hoc teams in achieving results, accountability for team performance (and the ability to assign team rewards) tends to be sporadic and uneven. And, as discussed throughout this book, without accountability for performance, attention will quickly be diverted to other tasks. There are too many competing demands.

Managers can create a stronger level of interaction when they form *permanent cross-unit teams*. Such permanent working groups might be charged with improving operating efficiency, enhancing responsiveness to customers, or interacting with key constituents. As with the ad hoc task forces, members of these permanent teams are drawn from different functions, product groups, and regions; but, in this case, the assignment is permanent.

Rather than rely on the informal support of a champion or cheerleader, the team now reports formally to a senior business leader, who in turn is responsible for the effectiveness of the team. As a result, accountability is stronger. For example, Merck— a pharmaceutical company organized functionally using the expert knowledge configuration—formed cross-functional worldwide business strategy teams for its major product categories. The mandate of each team was to focus on ways of competing more effectively by using brand marketing and competitive positioning to bring newly discovered and existing drugs to market. Each team reported formally to a member of the executive committee.[7]

Permanent cross-unit teams have the potential to fundamentally change interaction patterns and information exchange. Team members from a variety of market-facing and operating-core units bring their expertise, knowledge, and concerns to regular team meetings. Back in their home units, team members share agenda items that were developed in the cross-unit teams and help embed recommendations in unit goals and action plans. Thus, team members have wide spans of influence, bringing functional, regional, or product knowledge into the cross-unit team meetings and taking action items from the team back to their home units.

The chief executive officer of a consumer goods company described such an arrangement in his company:

> Every core team includes one member from each of four areas: marketing, design, finance, and manufacturing/engineering. The teams have global responsibility for their respective product lines and it's the cross-functional play that really makes them tick. Team members contribute from diverse perspectives to conceive, develop, price, and direct the marketing and merchandising of their products. Team heterogeneity promotes a good symmetry of design, engineering finesse, and marketing savvy that we might never achieve if we waited for isolated departments to bridge their efforts. Our teams work to optimize performance, profitability, development, and efficiency and thus ensure growth.[8]

Again, however, limitations in information technology and diagnostic control systems often constrain management's ability to set measurable team goals and evaluate team performance. Measures that are objective, complete, and responsive (the ideals discussed in chapter 4) are usually lacking. For example, the accounting system at Merck was not capable of calculating worldwide profit by product line. As a result, the effectiveness of the worldwide business strategy teams was limited by weak accountability for performance.

### Adding a Second Boss

Adding a second boss for individual positions is another approach for injecting creative tension. In a *dotted line reporting relationship*, a subordinate has two bosses (figure 5-5b). The primary boss manages the "solid line" accountability: the right to hire, fire, set goals, monitor performance, and allocate rewards. The secondary boss has weaker, dotted line accountability: the right to be consulted and provide input on goal setting and performance evaluation. For some professional jobs, such as accounting and legal services, the dotted line superior may also assume responsibility for professional training and career management.

Dotted line accountability can be found in any business and in any function. For example, in franchise restaurants such as KFC Corporation and Pizza Hut, dotted line accountability allows corporate operating-core managers to exert strong influence on regional operations:

> The corporate office of a [restaurant] chain was responsible for more than resource allocation and divisional performance evaluation; in practice, divisions had only limited autonomy. Indeed, the division heads of finance, marketing, human resources, and real estate had dotted line reporting relationships to the directors of each function in the corporate office. These dotted line relationships were very strong, essentially creating a centralized shadow hierarchy.[9]

In many companies, the accounting and finance function is managed with a dotted line structure. On the one hand, finance is expected to represent the interests of the corporate center: ensuring accuracy in reporting, compliance with corporate policies, and consistency in the application of accounting, performance measurement, and credit standards. This role is best fulfilled by organizing accounting and finance as a centrally managed operating-core function reporting to the corporation's chief financial officer. On the other hand, market-facing managers want the finance function to be an active member of their management team and assist with local performance manage-

ment systems, pricing and business development, and preparation of reports for corporate headquarters. From the perspective
of these local managers, responsiveness is key: accounting and
finance should report to them.

Because of this tension, senior managers must choose where
to draw the solid and dotted lines. One solution is illustrated in
figure 5-6.

In this design, the primary role of accounting and finance is
to ensure the integrity of controls and reporting. As a result, the
solid line reporting relationship is to the corporate controller
and CFO, who set performance goals and evaluate their regional
finance directors to ensure that corporate accounting and credit
policy standards are enforced consistently throughout the business. The weaker dotted line relationship is to the business unit
managers, who have the right to influence goal setting and evaluation but whose views are subordinated to the direct reporting
relationship to headquarters.

**FIGURE 5-6**

**Finance Organization: Solid Line to Center**

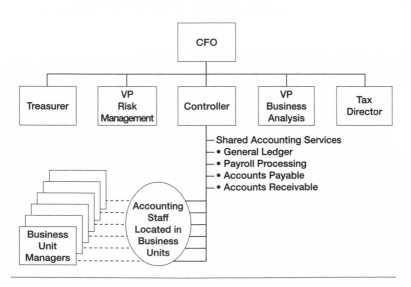

Alternatively, senior managers can reverse this relationship: accounting and finance can report directly to local unit managers, with weaker dotted line accountability to the corporate CFO. This choice would tilt the balance toward partnership with business unit managers. Although more responsive to the needs of market-facing managers, this design choice brings with it the danger that the regional accounting staff could be co-opted by their local bosses. As a result, finance personnel may be less vigilant in ensuring that colleagues on their local management team follow corporate reporting and credit policy guidelines—especially when market-facing units are under pressure to achieve tough performance targets.

Dotted line reporting relationships are not limited to staff groups such as accounting and human resources. Any position can have a secondary dotted line reporting relationship if senior managers think that the creative tension generated by a supplemental focus is important in building interactive networks and widening spans of influence. For example, a business unit product manager in Canada may report directly (solid line) to a global product head based in the United States, with a dotted line reporting relationship to the country manager for Canada.

In *matrix* reporting, the concept of adding a second boss is taken one step further. Under this arrangement, each subordinate has two equal bosses, both with solid line accountability (figure 5-5c). As with the dotted line reporting relationship, one boss may be responsible for a product group and another responsible for business performance in a country. But now, each boss has equal rights to set goals, monitor performance, and allocate compensation and incentives.

Taken to its logical extreme, some organizations may choose to organize their entire business using a matrix structure in which each unit reports simultaneously along two (or more) orthogonal dimensions that are some combination of function, product, geography, and customer. Similar to a matrix in mathematics with its array of columns and rows, a two-dimensional matrix—in this case organized by product and geography—is illustrated in figure 5-7.

Individuals at the intersection of these dual accountability structures must negotiate resource levels and performance goals with two bosses. As a result, interaction is very high. When conflicts in goals and priorities emerge, the two bosses must themselves negotiate an acceptable solution. Consequently, spans of influence throughout such an organization are extremely wide. People can accomplish little without reaching out for help to people in other units.

Matrix organizations place inordinate demands on information systems to support accountability. For example, one manager may need performance data by country, whereas a second manager requires worldwide performance data by product line. In such a case, a matrix organization design can work only if accounting and information technology systems allow the unified collection and distribution of data along regional as well as product dimensions.

It is extremely difficult to make a matrix organization work. But it can be done. In addition to information demands, strong norms must ensure that individuals are willing to negotiate and allocate resources in a way that can serve multiple agendas. Because matrix organizations are the ultimate test of organization design, I will have more to say about them in chapters 7 and 8. As you will see, a successful matrix design requires that all four levers of organization design are implemented and functioning properly.

## Using Accounting and Control Systems to Build Interactive Networks

In addition to these structural techniques, interactive networks can be built using accounting and control systems to do the following:

**FIGURE 5-7**

## Two-Dimensional Matrix Organization

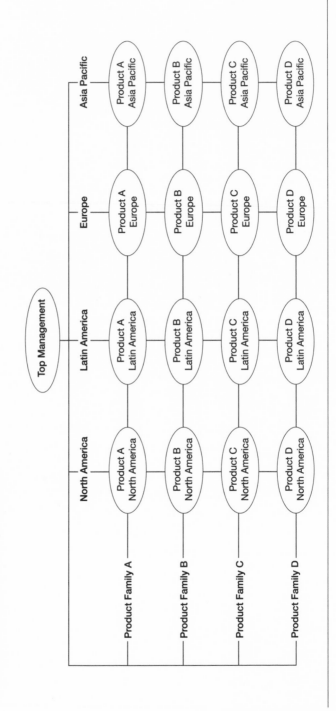

- Set demanding goals

- Allocate indirect costs

- Design transfer-pricing policies

### Setting Demanding Goals

"Ordinary goals inspire ordinary achievement."[10]

The literature on the art of setting performance goals is extensive, much of it arguing for bottom-up, participatory goal setting.[11] Research suggests that when subordinates participate in the goal-setting process, goals not only are more likely to be realistic but also are seen as valid and legitimate, thereby increasing employee commitment. According to this wisdom, performance goals should be set at levels that are challenging but achievable. If goals are too easy, they will fail to provide needed motivation; conversely, if goals are so difficult that they are seen as unachievable, individuals will lose hope and give up.

Notwithstanding this seemingly sound advice, anyone who has worked in a high-performing organization knows that senior managers often set unilateral, top-down goals that are so demanding as to seem unreasonable. To achieve these goals requires both extraordinary effort and some measure of luck. GE's former CEO, Jack Welch, described stretch targets as "using dreams to set business targets, with no real idea of how to get there."[12] But there may be good reason for this approach, which injects considerable tension into any organization. BP CEO John Browne explains:

> To get people to learn, you need to give them a challenge. Setting a target is crucial even if you don't actually know whether it's fully achievable—because in times of rapid change, you have to make decisions and get people to step outside the box.

One process that we employ to promote learning and drive performance is not that unusual. It involves understanding the critical measures of operating performance in each business, relentlessly benchmarking those measures and their related activities, setting higher and higher targets, and challenging people to achieve them.[13]

When facing difficult targets, people often respond in surprisingly creative ways, following what one executive described as the "cornered rat" theory of management. To have any chance of success, employees must think creatively to obtain resources or influence people who control the resources they need. To succeed, they must widen their span of influence, relying on a network of peers and contacts from different regions—key account managers, product managers, marketing managers, sales field managers, and finance managers—to accomplish their goals.

Information technology often plays a critical role in this process. To support learning, BP implemented a "knowledge management" framework that relied heavily on an information technology infrastructure to support knowledge sharing worldwide.[14] Intranets, electronic blackboards, and virtual team networks were used extensively to allow people throughout the organization to participate in and influence activities that led to the successful achievement of shared goals.[15]

In applying these techniques, there is one critical caveat. When managers knowingly create performance pressure through stretch goals, there should always be an escape valve for failure. It is important, for example, to add contingency lines to budgets and to reset performance evaluations to reflect honest effort. In this way, individuals do not have to feel that they must engage in unethical or damaging behavior to achieve their goals. In addition, managers must ensure that strong levers of control in place. Belief systems should emphasize honesty, integrity, and investment for the long term. Senior managers must also communicate business conduct and strategic boundaries to prohibit unethical behavior or unsound business practices. Such proscriptions must be unambiguous and enforced consistently. Finally, internal accounting controls must be strong: segregation of duties, top management reviews and authorization of transactions, and independent audits must be in place and enforced to ensure that any indiscretion or error is quickly detected.[16]

### Allocating Indirect Costs

Cost accounting may seem like an odd topic for organization design, but skillful managers know that the tools of cost allocation can be surprisingly effective as a means of fostering interactive networks and of widening span of influence.

When indirect costs (e.g., depreciation, central R&D, and general overheads that do not vary directly with volume) are charged from one unit to another, managers at the receiving end pay careful attention to the choices made by managers responsible for generating those costs. For example, consider what happens when administration costs from corporate headquarters are allocated to manufacturing plants. If plant managers, who must add these costs to their product costs, feel that the level of corporate spending is excessive, they have strong incentives to voice their concern, applying pressure to the corporate managers who originate those costs to economize or consider options such as outsourcing.

In a field study of a computer firm that used such cost allocations to foster creative tension, Dent quotes a finance manager who described how the system widened span of influence: "It encourages dialogue. Development units want to know what the territories are spending their money on. Sales territories want to know what development units are spending their money on. It creates reciprocal pressure."[17]

The widely accepted *controllability principle* states that a manager should not be held accountable for performance that he or she cannot control.[18] However, there are important exceptions. If managers want to widen span of influence and promote creative thinking, they should in fact assign costs that managers do not fully control.

In a study of decentralized companies, Richard Vancil amplifies this point:

> The cost responsibilities of a profit center manager always exceed the local costs of his functional resources to a greater or lesser extent. Corporate managers use the calculation of profit to influence the behavior of each profit center manager, and the message they are sending to him in deciding to assign the costs of shared resources is that the scope of his initiative should not be restricted solely to the resources for which he has functional authority. A profit center manager shares resources that are also utilized by others, and his responsibility includes trying to influence the management of those shared resources. . . . Assigning, or failing to assign, cost responsibility for shared resources tells a profit center manager what to worry about; the method of cost assignment, in effect, tells him how much to worry.[19]

Of course, the creative tension introduced by such techniques depends on the relative importance of indirect costs in the value chain. In firms where indirect costs are a large percentage of overall costs, managers will pay a great deal of attention to the level and accuracy of cost allocations. To augment creative tension, some firms allocate a cost of capital charge to all units based on the assets under their control. For firms where indirect costs are either a minor proportion of overall costs or outside a manager's span of accountability, the level of creative tension introduced by these systems will be small.

To be effective in widening span of influence, cost allocations must be perceived as fair and valid. If they are not, managers will either ignore allocations (with predictable complaints and grumbling) or will dissipate energy in attempts to resolve the inequity. Consider a firm where senior managers decided to allocate all indirect costs to products using a simple averaging method. Accountants simply added up all the overhead costs ($X$) and divided this sum by the number of units produced ($n$). By simple division, each unit of product was then allocated indirect costs equal to $(X/n)$.

Unfortunately, because this firm had multiple products and customers, allocating costs based on a simple volume measure led to a misallocation of costs. Complex products with demanding customers used a relatively high amount of indirect resources. But these products bore the same per-unit overhead charges as simple products that required relatively little administrative support and overhead costs. As a result, the former products were undercosted and the latter overcosted, leading to higher profitability for some business units and lower profits for others. Not surprisingly, managers spent a good deal of their time arguing about the inaccuracies of the cost allocations.

A well-designed *activity-based costing system* remedies this problem by tracing indirect costs to activities and products in proportion to their actual consumption. As a result, managers can rely on the validity of the cost allocations and can devote their energies to either managing costs more effectively or influencing the managers who make decisions about resource levels and utilization.

### Designing Transfer-Pricing Policies

Over the years, a great deal has been written on transfer pricing in the accounting and economics literature.[20] Drawing heavily on mathematical programming models, this literature has focused almost exclusively on devising systems that motivate unit managers to make value-creating decisions in the absence of any discussion between them. Little has been written, however, on the role of transfer pricing in widening span of influence.

When products are shipped internally from an upstream unit to a downstream unit, the transfer price determines the revenue and costs of the respective units. Transfer prices can be set according to a number of accounting formulas (figure 5-8). If the upstream division is a cost center, then the transfer price will likely be limited to variable costs, or variable costs plus an allocation of indirect overheads. If the sending division is a profit center, then the transfer price will add a profit margin to acknowledge the value added by the upstream division. Of course, the higher the revenue to the upstream unit, the higher the cost to the receiving unit—and the lower its profit.

Because transfer-pricing policies shift costs and profits between organizational units, managers will attempt to influence their counterparts in other units to ensure that their interests are protected. Transfer prices set at standard variable cost are unlikely to attract much attention because the transfer price will

**FIGURE 5-8**

**Hierarchy of Transfer-Pricing Formulas**

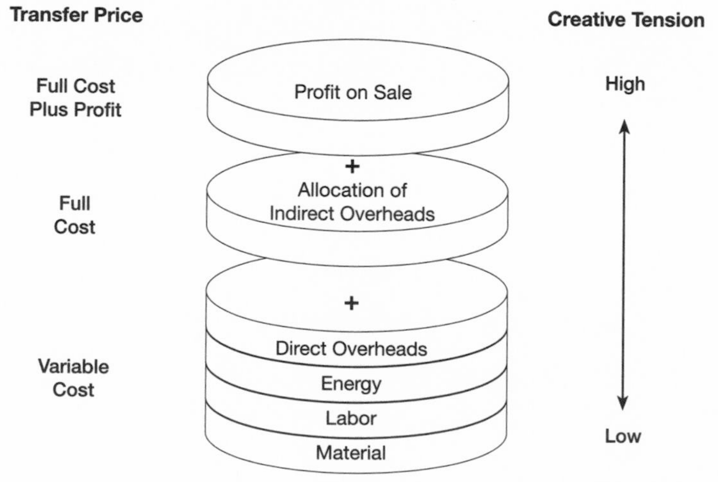

likely be lower than any alternative source of supply.[21] Downstream managers will become much more interested, however, if overhead costs, volume variances, and profit are added to the transfer price. Every dollar of cost or profit added by the upstream division becomes a dollar of lost profit for the receiving unit. Strong incentives now exist for the receiving division to influence the operations of the upstream division to ensure that good business practices are keeping the cost of goods transferred as low as possible.

One of my students, trained as a chemical engineer, noted, "When I was at ExxonMobil, we were constantly simulating the management of the inflows and outflows of product between chemical plants and refineries. The transfer pricing was used to generate creative tension between the chemical plant and refinery. This had a strategic purpose—to encourage the chemical plant and refinery to find ways to work together to achieve maximum production at the lowest possible cost for both."[22]

To maximize creative tension, senior managers can give units the right to purchase from outside suppliers rather than accept higher-cost internal transfers. Depending on internal cost structures and capacity constraints, such systems can generate significant pressures to lower costs or increase revenues or both. For example, the upstream division may be allowed to divert its goods or services for sale in outside markets if it can realize higher prices. Similarly, the downstream unit may be allowed to decline internal transfers in favor of cheaper outside sources.[23]

Of course, the allocation of indirect costs and the use of transfer-pricing policies are not ends in themselves. Instead, as illustrated in figure 5-9, these techniques are triggers for cross-unit interaction and influence. We might call this the CIIO approach: costs in, influence out. In principle, the more that indirect costs and profits are transferred between units with wide spans of accountability, the more that managers will attempt to influence the managers of the units generating those costs.

**FIGURE 5-9**

## Widening Span of Influence: Costs in, Influence Out

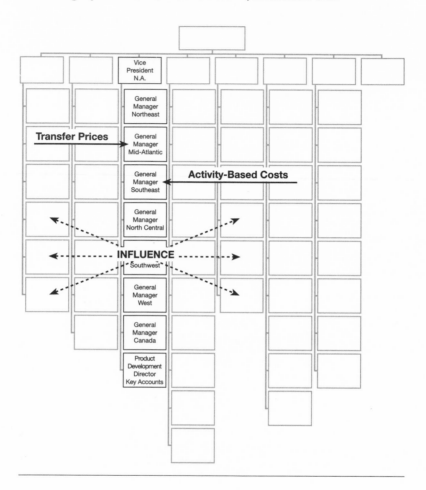

# FOCUSING ATTENTION ON
# STRATEGIC UNCERTAINTIES

In a dynamic competitive environment, managers may want to focus attention throughout their entire organization on the strategic uncertainties associated with specific strategies. The mechanisms described here are intended to widen spans of influence and encourage information sharing and interaction among market-facing and operating-core units. But interactive networks need not be only horizontal between units; they can also be vertical, drawing superiors and subordinates into frequent dialogue, debate, and action planning. A simple, powerful principle underlies this approach: the maxim that everyone watches what the boss watches. Like a waterfall, management attention cascades down from the top of the organization. So the critical question becomes, "What information is the boss watching?"

The answer to this question defines interactive control systems. *Interactive control systems* are the information systems that managers use to involve themselves regularly and personally in the decision activities of subordinates.[24] Interactive control systems are the hot buttons of senior managers—the information that they watch regularly and discuss constantly with subordinates.

To make a control system interactive, four conditions are necessary:

1. Information generated by the system must be a consistently important agenda for the highest levels of management.

2. As a result of top management's ongoing interest, data reported by the system receives frequent and regular attention from operating managers at all levels of the organization.

3. Data generated is discussed in face-to-face meetings of superiors, subordinates, and peers.

4. The focus of the discussion is the challenge and debate of data, assumptions, and action plans.[25]

Managers can use any control system interactively if they so choose. For example, a study of thirty businesses in the health-care industry revealed that senior managers, through their personal focus and attention, used one of five control systems interactively:

- Project monitoring systems

- Profit planning systems

- Brand revenue systems

- Intelligence systems

- Human development systems[26]

Depending on the industry and the preferences of senior managers, this list could be expanded to include balanced scorecards, customer satisfaction systems, or any other systems that top managers choose to focus on.

It is important to understand that the same system—whether a profit plan, a market share rating report, or a balanced scorecard—can be used either diagnostically or interactively. Diagnostic control systems are management-by-exception systems. No news is good news. If strategy implementation is on track, no further follow-up is required. Interactive systems, in contrast, are the hot buttons of senior management. The goal of using any control system interactively is to identify emerging changes in the business—both positive and negative surprises—that may require changing the business model or strategy. In short, diagnostic systems are used for control; interactive systems are used primarily for learning.

When senior managers use a control system interactively, subordinates throughout the business anticipate that they will be challenged in face-to-face meetings—to offer explanations and action plans in response to emerging information and trends. A senior manager at Pepsi, for example, described how he and his colleagues used a weekly market share data system interactively:

> Pepsi's top managers would carry little charts in their wallets with the latest key Nielsen figures. They became such an important part of my life that I could quote them on any

product in any market. We would pore over the data using it to search for Coke's vulnerable points where an assault could successfully be launched, or to explore why Pepsi slipped a fraction of a percentage point in the game. . . . The Nielsens defined the ground rules of competition for everyone at Pepsi. They were at the epicenter of all we did. They were the non-public body counts of the Cola Wars. . . . The company wasn't always this way. The man at the front of the table made it so.[27]

At Pepsi, the author added,

No matter where I was at any time of the day, when the Nielsen flash came out, I wanted to be the first to know about it. I didn't mind a problem, but I hated surprises. The last thing I'd want was [Pepsi's CEO] calling for an explanation behind a weak number without having had the chance to see it myself. I'd scribble the details down on the back of an envelope. . . . Within an hour, some sixty or seventy people at Pepsi also would get the results and begin to work on them.[28]

This interactive process is illustrated in figure 5-10. The current business strategy—how the business creates value for customers and differentiates its products and services from competitors—is represented at the upper left. But no strategy can be left untended for long. What are the competitive issues that keep senior managers awake at night? Is it competitor challenges, changes in technology, or shifting customer demographics? These strategic uncertainties must constantly be monitored to ensure that the organization is adapting to changing conditions.

To focus the entire organization on these strategic uncertainties, senior managers make one (or a very small number of)

**FIGURE 5-10**

## Interactive Control Process

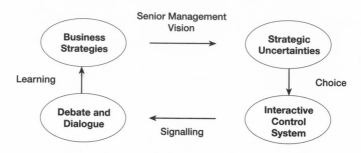

*Source:* Simons, *Levers of Control:* 102. Reprinted by permission of the Harvard Business School Press.

control systems interactive. Their personal attention to a performance measurement system generates creative tension throughout the business. Everyone in the organization watches what the boss watches—a profit plan, a balanced scorecard, or, as with Pepsi, a brand revenue system—and attempts to formulate responses to the inevitable questions that will arise in face-to-face meetings with senior management.

As top managers review data, probe for new information, and challenge subordinates, interactive networks are built up naturally in the organization. In anticipation of meetings with superiors, subordinates gather their own information and test action plans, cutting across organizational boundaries when necessary.

From this highly interactive debate and dialogue, new ideas often emerge. Sometimes, this process lays the seeds for new strategies. At *USA Today*, such an interactive process was instrumental in developing many of the innovations (e.g., fractional four-color advertisements, regional ads, and freestanding inserts) that allowed the newspaper to flourish and reshape the entire industry.[29]

## INCENTIVES TO SUPPORT
## INTERACTIVE NETWORKS

Incentives, if not properly designed, can easily derail the desired benefits of interactive networks. For example, if bonuses are based solely on local unit performance, then managers may waste time arguing over transfer prices and cost allocations. More insidiously, they may try to game the system by manipulating data or biasing information to make their unit's performance appear better. In a worst-case, winner-take-all strategy, managers may attempt to sabotage the performance of other managers or units to enhance their own reported performance.

This unfortunate result occurred in a chemical company that transferred semifinished goods from its Canadian plant to a sister plant in Belgium. The manager of the Antwerp plant consistently promised to take more output than he actually did. Because of the cost allocation and transfer-pricing policies, this shortfall consistently created a negative volume variance that reduced the profit of the Canadian plant. Because the managers of these two plants were in competition for a senior-level promotion, some observers questioned whether the European manager was gaming the system to reduce the profit of his rival and improve the relative performance of his own unit.[30]

Incentives can help overcome this type of problem. One approach is to base a substantial potion of incentive compensation on group profit rather than on the results of individual profit centers. At the limit, rewards can be linked to overall corporate performance so that managers are more concerned with the success of the whole than the parochial interests of their particular units.

This solution was adopted at General Motors when senior managers discovered that the Chevrolet division was earning more money selling cars internally to Pontiac than on cars it sold to its own external customers. As a result of this distortion, overall financial performance of the corporation was suffering. The solution was to make North America the sole profit center. The head of North American operations said, "We've tried to get around the allocation and transfer pricing issues and get a clear glimpse from the market of what price we can sell a particular vehicle for." GM's CEO stated, "Now the only profit center is North America, where all resources and functions are concentrated. The leaders of each area of the vehicle business are working toward the common goal of positive financial results for all of North America rather than the individual units."[31]

Of course, this solution eliminates the potential benefits that may arise from properly designed cost allocations and transfer pricing. For this reason, managers at the Canadian chemical plant referred to earlier chose to maintain their transfer-pricing system even though they were aware of the potential for abuse, stating that they wanted managers to be aware of the volume variance, which was dragging down group profit. Above all else, they wanted to keep spans of influence wide so that managers throughout the corporation would be worrying about the costs of excess capacity and attempting to find creative solutions as well as influence others who could help solve the problem.

A second approach to incentives is to base a substantial portion of incentives on subjective evaluation—often supported by a 360-degree performance evaluation process. Assessment of an individual's effort, initiative, and willingness to share information across organizational boundaries can then become an important input for evaluation and reward. This is especially important for the interactive control systems discussed here. However, this solution is costly. For subjective evaluation to be perceived as fair, it is essential that superiors invest sufficient time and resources to fully understand the conditions, choices, and efforts of the individual being evaluated. Managers must therefore invest substantial effort to understand the effort and contribution of different individuals in generating information and ideas as part of the interactive process.[32]

## REVISITING STRATEGY

All these techniques inject tension into an organization in one way or another. The intent, of course, is to make the tension creative and to force people to think outside the box. But any design choice brings with it tradeoffs and potential risks. The techniques described in this chapter force individuals to move out of their comfort zones and split their attention into multiple directions. When you force managers to focus attention on the work of other units, you divert scarce management resources from their prime tasks and accountabilities. As one manager stated, "It's as if my 'day job' is managing my own business, and my 'night job' is ensuring that I'm collaborating with the rest of the company."[33]

A balance must be struck between, on the one hand, creative tension, interactive networks, and a wide span of influence and, on the other, the clarity that comes from line-of-sight accountability. Confusion cannot be allowed to overwhelm the implementation of current strategies. No firm can survive if it cannot generate adequate financial returns—profit, cash flow, and return on capital employed.

Thus, managers must analyze strategy carefully to determine the desired level of creative tension and spans of influence. In rapidly changing, dynamic markets, a high level of creative tension may be essential for successful long-term competition. People must be motivated to constantly look for new ways of creating value for customers and responding to competitive threats. In slower-moving, less demanding industries, such rapid response may be unnecessary and needlessly disruptive. In these circumstances, managers may choose to narrow spans of influence and avoid interactive networks. The focus on defined tasks to achieve current goals is more important than creative learning and longer-term adaptation.

## AVOIDING DESTRUCTIVE TENSION

For an organization to function effectively with wide spans of influence and productive interactive networks, a variety of complex interpersonal skills become essential. Individuals must learn how to cross boundaries, build alliances, manage conflict, and communicate effectively.[34] Certain influence tactics are more prevalent than others. One research study found, for example, that when individuals attempt to influence others from whom they need support, the frequency of tactics can be ranked as follows:

1. Consultation to encourage participation

2. Persuasion through presentation of logical arguments

3. Inspirational appeals

4. Ingratiating tactics

5. Formation of coalitions to persuade key individuals

6. Pressure and implied threats

7. Upward appeals for assistance

8. Promise of reciprocal exchange or favor[35]

Some of these tactics will be more productive than others in creating positive dialogue through interactive networks. Managers must ensure that influence skills do not devolve into politicking and other behaviors that are detrimental to the achievement of organizational goals and strategies. Instead, managers must create an environment where people feel safe in reaching out to build and exploit interactive networks. To facilitate positive interaction, managers may need to invest in training and job rotation.

*Psychological safety* is the degree to which individuals perceive their work environment as conducive to interpersonal risk-taking. When work environments are psychologically safe, people believe that an unintended mistake will not result in punishment or disapproval. What's more, they know that others will not resent or punish them for asking for help, information, or feedback. As a result, people feel secure in taking risks and can be more open to learning.[36]

At Honda, for example, employees and superiors are encouraged to ignore hierarchy in institutionalized brainstorming sessions called *waigaya*, which means, "Say whatever." Someone who has worked in this environment noted the following:

> Waigaya can only be attained if there is a safe environment for employees to express their opinions without fearing future penalties in terms of promotion opportunity and compensation. In order to make waigaya work, Honda evaluates how much each individual has encouraged waigaya as an important criterion for managerial promotions.[37]

In addition to specific skill development, job rotation can allow individuals to appreciate the challenges of other units. Scientists and administrative staff can visit customers to learn more about product and competitive issues. Staff can be cross-trained so that they can perform a wide range of duties (as is done at, for example, Southwest Airlines and Starbucks). As people spend time together, influence networks flourish as personal friendships and trust are created through shared experiences.

## TECHNOLOGY TO SUPPORT
## INTERACTIVE NETWORKS

The ability of people to interact across organizational boundaries has never been greater. Communication technology continues to evolve at a rapid pace: e-mail, text messaging, video-
conferencing, and wireless communications have all become
commonplace. Such means of communicating are an essential
ingredient in influence networks.

When General Motors decided to build its new Equinox
SUV at a factory in Ontario with engines built in China, four
countries cooperated in the design:

> From a dimly lit "global collaboration room" just outside
> Toronto, engineers teleconferenced almost daily with coun-
> terparts in Shanghai; Mitaka, Japan; and Warren, Mich.
> They swapped virtual-reality renderings of the vehicle and
> collaborated on the styling of exteriors and design of com-
> ponents. This year, GM bought an IBM supercomputer to
> make such collaboration even faster. The result was the
> Chevrolet Equinox, which enjoyed a successful start in the
> U.S. market.[38]

In addition to these high-tech innovations, we must remember that dual accountability structures must be supported by underlying accounting systems that can collect and aggregate data
along each dimension of accountability (e.g., by unit, function,
product, region, or customer). Computing infrastructures and
accounting systems must be in place to support activity-based
cost systems and transfer-pricing systems. If the accounting systems and IT infrastructures are inadequate, it will be difficult to
implement interactive networks effectively.

In addition, notwithstanding the importance of technology, managers at DuPont remind us that often there is no substitute for face-to-face interaction:

> At DuPont, we consider networks essential tools of innovation, and we encourage them in every way—including financially. We go to great lengths to ensure that everyone knows about existing networks, and we publicize their achievement. . . . Although two-thirds of our research networking today is electronic, face-to-face contacts are critical. There's no way to equal the synergy that develops when gifted people are in a room together."[39]

### CHAPTER THEME

Managers can motivate subordinates to build networks of interaction and influence.

### KEY CHAPTER IDEAS

- A critical task of leadership is to inject creative tension to counterbalance the natural forces of stability that are created by vertical hierarchy and diagnostic control systems.

- *Definition:* Interactive networks are the structures and systems that stimulate individuals to gather information and influence the decisions of others.

- *Definition:* Span of influence defines the width of the net that an individual casts in collecting data, probing for new information, and attempting to influence the work of others.

- Managers widen span of influence by creating interactive networks that draw together people from different units and force individuals to think out of the box and learn.

- Interactive networks can be created through dual influence structures that force individuals to split their attention in two or more directions by
  - Adding an overlay of secondary activities
  - Adding a second boss

- Interactive networks can also be created by the use of accounting and control systems to create pressure to pay attention to activities in other units or positions by
  - Setting span of accountability greater than span of control
  - Setting demanding goals
  - Allocating indirect costs
  - Designing transfer-pricing policies
  - Using control systems interactively

- Matrix organizations can work, but only if all four levers of organization design are finely tuned and implemented properly.

## ACTION STEPS

1. Based on your organization's strategy and structure, determine the desired levels of creative tension for different units and key management positions.

2. If needed, widen spans of influence for various positions by using the following techniques:

**FIGURE 5-11**

## Lever 3: Interactive Networks

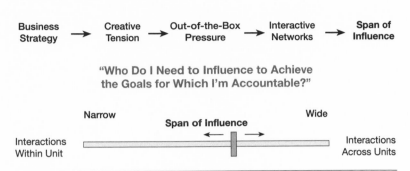

Business Strategy → Creative Tension → Out-of-the-Box Pressure → Interactive Networks → Span of Influence

"Who Do I Need to Influence to Achieve the Goals for Which I'm Accountable?"

Narrow — Span of Influence — Wide

Interactions Within Unit ←|→ Interactions Across Units

a. Create interactive networks by designing dual influence structures:
  • Cross-functional teams
  • Dotted line reporting relationships
  • Matrix accountability
b. Create interactive networks by using accounting and control systems:
  • Set span of accountability greater than span of control.
  • Set stretch goals.
  • Use activity-based cost systems and transfer pricing to increase span of influence.
  • Use control systems interactively.

3. Clarify solid and dotted line reporting relationships for the accounting and finance function.

# 6

---

# SHARED RESPONSIBILITIES

THE PREVIOUS THREE CHAPTERS introduced the first three levers of organization design: unit structure, diagnostic control systems, and interactive networks. We modeled our approach on the stages followed by an architect designing a building: analyzing existing conditions and topography, laying out the dimensions and shape of the foundation, designing the structures and room dividers, configuring the energy systems and wiring, and ensuring that the traffic flow between rooms achieves the desired results.

In this chapter, we undertake the final step: ensuring that the right people occupy the building. The ideas presented in this chapter—focusing on group norms, leadership, and responsibility—typically are not central topics of organization design. But the traits of the people who make up an organization are as much a design variable as the other organization features we have discussed.

There is a vigorous debate in business schools about the inherent nature of people in organizations. Economists, interested primarily in the functioning of markets, assume that individuals are self-interested and work to maximize their own economic well-being, even if it entails shirking and biasing information. Social scientists trained in psychology, sociology, and organization behavior take a different view. They argue that intrinsic motivation—for example, satisfaction from a job well done—is a more powerful animator of human behavior.

Of course, different assumptions about human behavior lead to very different design approaches. For economists, organization design focuses primarily on decision rights, contracts, and the financial rewards that align, monitor, and discipline self-interested behavior. For social scientists who specialize in individual emotions and group dynamics, the importance of psychological factors leads to a focus on intrinsic motivation, affiliation, and group norms.

I will not debate the merits or take a position regarding the reasonableness of these differing views; each has something to offer. However, it is important to note that both approaches take human behavior as a given. In other words, the nature of human beings in organizations is treated as an exogenous variable—a constraint that predetermines available design choices.

I take a different tack. Rather than accept human nature as an exogenous constraint, I view it as an endogenous *choice variable* in the design of organizations. Thus, a critical task of senior managers is to decide how they wish individuals to act in their organization and then create the necessary conditions for them to act in the desired ways.

The key assumption of this chapter, then, is that human behavior can, and should, be molded to suit particular strategies and organization designs. I will attempt to answer a question posed by organizational scholar Charles Perrow: "Under what conditions will people in organizations maximize their own utilities regardless of the consequences for others, and when will they forgo an increase in utility or even suffer a loss because of the consequences for others?"[1]

## COMMITMENT TO OTHERS

It is now time to introduce our final C: *commitment to others* (see figure 6-1). As with the other Cs, managers must analyze and determine the level of commitment to others that is needed to support their organization's strategy. Then they must adjust the final lever—shared responsibilities—to ensure the appropriate level of commitment. Commitment to others focuses on strategy as perspective: how people interpret the rights and responsibilities of their organizational world and their relationship with the other individuals who work around them.

**FIGURE 6-1**

**Lever 4: Shared Responsibilities**

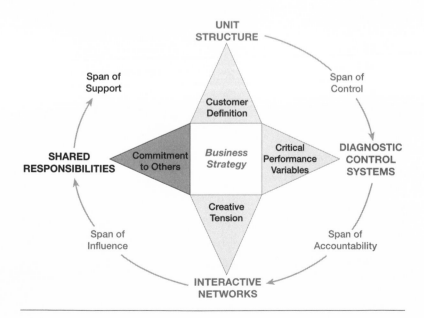

Commitment to others takes two basic forms. The most basic manifestation is a willingness to exert effort to assist other people in achieving their goals, even if there is no personal gain—or sometimes even personal cost—to those offering such support. When commitment to others is strong, individuals are willing to divert their energy and attention from their own agenda to assist someone else. The person needing assistance may be someone in another unit, a subordinate, or a superior. To this end, Andy Grove, past CEO of Intel, told his employees that he wanted them to display the same commitment and dedicated teamwork that emergency workers demonstrate when responding to natural disasters, putting aside self-interest and territoriality for cooperation and mutual support.[2]

Commitment to others can also be found in a willingness to proactively share information that may be useful to other people or other units. In such circumstances, individuals are thinking actively about the goals of others and are willing to take time away from their personal agenda to convey information that may assist in the achievement of the other's goals. Again, there is often no immediate payoff (and sometimes a cost) for those offering such information.

The extent to which people feel commitment to help others varies dramatically across organizations. Consider two very different organizations: the U.S. Marine Corps and the Wall Street trading floor of a large brokerage house.

In the Marines, the primary duty of each individual is to help the person beside him. This culture is deeply ingrained through explicit edict, intensive training, and indoctrination. To reinforce the importance of this duty, highly valued recognition is bestowed with great ceremony on those who exemplify a willingness to lay self-interest aside to help others in peril.

By contrast, the primary duty of a Wall Street trader is to make money for his trading desk (and himself). Acting primarily as free agents, traders have neither an expectation nor a responsibility to help anyone else on the trading floor or in other units of the firm. It is every man (or woman) for himself.

These norms of behavior are not inherently right or wrong—just different, and each is entirely appropriate to the organization's unique strategies and circumstances. In the impersonal, market-based trading floor, there is good reason to create an organization predicated on self-interest. Each individual attempts to identify market imperfections and exploit arbitrage opportunities in a zero-sum game of market winners and losers. Self-interest stimulates the hunt for private information, risk taking, and the generation of wealth: there is little need to engender a willingness to help others.

In the Marines, by contrast, concerted team effort is essential for success. In battle, with an enemy attempting to divide and conquer, total commitment to help others in distress is critical. Norms must be created by which individuals are willing to put their lives on the line with the knowledge that others will help and support them. Such behavior ensures that tactical missions will succeed regardless of unanticipated obstacles in rapidly changing circumstances. In an address that emphasized this point, Lawrence Summers, president of Harvard University, noted that soldiers on the battlefield do not give their lives for their country. They give their lives to help fellow soldiers in trouble—to pull them out of a trench under enemy fire.[3]

With any altruistic or noble trait, it would seem that more is better: creating a commitment to help others is always a good thing. Like any design variable, however, this behavior has costs that must be weighed carefully. In the Marines, the cost may be the ultimate sacrifice:

> In his book, *Administrative Behavior*, Herbert Simon discusses
> a pointed example of two very different forms of identification:

"Two soldiers sit in a trench opposite a machine-gun nest. One of them stays under cover. The other, at the cost of his life, destroys the machine-gun nest with a grenade. Which is rational?" Obviously Simon's question is not meant to be answered. What can be said is that under the circumstances one individual opted for his personal goals while the other exhibited a strong identification with those of his organization.[4]

In most organizations the cost of helping others is not this high. Nevertheless, there are still opportunity costs to consider. Even in the relative safety of modern business organizations, people who help others are invariably pulled away from their own agendas and may, as a result, be distracted from their work.

How do managers decide on the necessary level of commitment to others? In some circumstances, commitment to help others must be high to ensure success; in other circumstances, it can be set low. In part, this choice will be influenced by the personal style and preferences of senior leaders. But more fundamentally, it will be determined by business strategy and structure, especially by choices regarding customer loyalty and the complexity of the organization design.

## Customer Loyalty

In many companies—including exclusive hotel chains (Ritz-Carlton), low-cost service-oriented airlines (Southwest Airlines), and organizations that compete using a dedicated service relationship configuration (IBM or Siebel Systems)—achieving customer loyalty is critical for the implementation of strategy. In such organizations, commitment to helping others is essential to long-term success.

To achieve and sustain customer loyalty, employees must be willing to routinely step outside their job descriptions to anticipate and satisfy customer needs—whether it involves meeting a guest's unusual service requests, turning a plane around on time, or developing a novel technology solution that bundles products and services from different units. To respond to customer needs, individuals must be willing to assist others who are attempting to respond to customer requests or must overcome obstacles that could interfere with effective delivery of services. Satisfying customers becomes more important than staying within the confines of job descriptions.

In contrast, commitment to others is much less important in organizations that transact in open markets with transparent pricing. Because supply and demand is met through impersonal markets, customer loyalty is less critical. For example, in organizations such as commodity trading firms or used car auction wholesalers, individuals act as free agents using proprietary information to extract value in a competitive marketplace. Commission-based incentives are generally sufficient to motivate behaviors that create wealth for employees as well as the employing organization.

We can generalize: when employee responsiveness is an essential ingredient of strategy, commitment to help others who are working toward the same shared goal—customer loyalty— becomes critical. On the flip side of the coin, the closer a firm is aligned to liquid and efficient markets, the more the firm itself can be organized like a market. Commitment to others becomes less important.

## Design Complexity

Commitment to help others also becomes important for organizations that have complex value chains and structures. Chapter 5 discussed how managers can motivate individuals to think creatively and cross organizational boundaries by building dual influence structures such as cross-functional task teams, dotted line accountability, and matrix reporting structures. However, installing these interactive networks makes any organization much more complex as its parts multiply and become more interdependent. To operate successfully, individuals in these complex organizations must be willing to work with people in other units. Decision outcomes must be negotiated, goals must be reconciled, and work must be coordinated. Commitment to others must be high as people respond to requests for help.

Complexity can also arise from sophisticated production technologies and customer interfaces. Such complexity often results from what are called sequential and reciprocal interdependencies.[5]

These concepts are illustrated in figure 6-2.

In *sequential interdependence*, the output of one group serves as input to another group. For example, different manufacturing plants may supply a variety of raw materials and intermediate products to a finishing plant. With this sequential interdependence, managers must carefully schedule coordination to avoid

**FIGURE 6-2**

## Sequential and Reciprocal Interdependencies

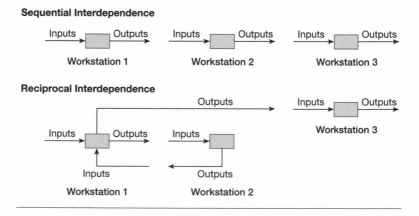

stock-outs and bottlenecks. Individuals from different units must work together to ensure effective coordination.

*Reciprocal interdependence* represents a higher order of complexity. In this case, one group completes the first stage of its work and then transfers materials or products to a second group. After the second group has completed its tasks, the work-in-process is sent back to the first group for additional processing. In an automotive company, for example, the power train engineering group delivers an engine prototype to both the manufacturing and the design groups. The design group uses the prototype to determine suspension alignment and key dimensions for the engine compartment and hood shape; the manufacturing group assesses the tooling that will be needed for factory production. Both groups then go back to the power train engineers with requests for modifications to accommodate either sheet metal design or manufacturing capabilities.

Reciprocal interdependencies are common in highly complex, integrative work systems that rely on technical engineering to build aircraft and space systems (such as Boeing and Lockheed Martin) and in sophisticated financial services firms (such as Citigroup and Goldman Sachs). Because of the complex task integration required in these firms to bring products and services to market, individuals must be willing to offer support when requested—and to be proactive in reaching out when they believe that their assistance would help achieve organizational goals.

Although basic coordination can be achieved by the structures and systems described in previous chapters, complex product systems cannot function effectively if individuals work myopically without regard to the needs of customers or those working in other units. This is especially true when people working in specialized technical units (e.g., engineering, finance, marketing) may feel more loyalty to their subgroups and professional disciplines than they do to the overriding mission of the organization. In such circumstances, the response "That's not my job" becomes a recipe for organizational gridlock.

## SPAN OF SUPPORT

Based on their unique strategies and circumstances, different organizations—the Marines, a Wall Street trading firm, or a consumer goods company—require different levels of commitment to others. As a result, individuals in any organization need to know the answer to a critical question: "How much support can I expect when I reach out to others for help in achieving my goals?" The answer to this question defines *span of support*: the range of support that an individual can anticipate and expect from people in other organizational units. The flip side of this question is, "Who do I need to help to ensure their success in our shared mission?"

This definition reminds us again that organization design is intended primarily to influence the work and attention of individuals. Accordingly, span of support, like the other spans, is defined first at the individual level and can range from narrow to wide.

By treating human behavior as a design variable, we now introduce an additional slider that can be adjusted to balance the other three spans from earlier chapters. Figure 6-3 illustrates span of support for a global marketing manager in an international food company organized according to the local value creation configuration.

As indicated by the relatively narrow span of control, this manager controls few of the resources needed for success: she does not control product design in the individual countries, nor does she regulate regional advertising programs and budgets. Yet her span of accountability is relatively wide. Sales volume,

**FIGURE 6-3**

## Organization Design Sliders—Global Marketing Manager

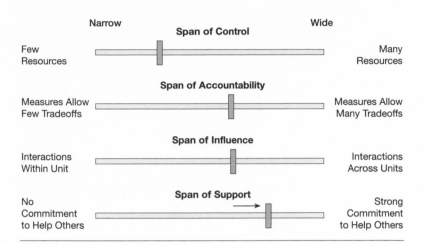

market share, and price premiums are all important indicators of global marketing success in the markets for which she is accountable.

Because her span of accountability is greater than her span of control, an entrepreneurial gap exists. Her span of influence is also relatively wide, reflecting extensive interactive networks that senior managers have created in the organization. Important marketing initiatives, for example, are launched via cross-unit task forces that include regional managers, functional managers, and global marketing managers. In addition, dotted line accountability links global marketing directors to the regions.

With so few resources and so many demands, the marketing director must feel confident that others will step forward, when asked, to support initiatives that may not impact their jobs directly. To succeed, her span of support must be wide.

Span of support can differ across units and positions. For example, in the previous chapter we described a number of structural techniques for building interactive networks: ad hoc cross-unit teams, dotted line reporting relationships, and matrix structures. To ensure widespread support for these mechanisms, senior managers are often designated as champions or are given direct responsibility for ensuring that these overlays of supplemental activities work effectively. In such cases, managers must use their personal attention to signal to others in the organization the importance of supporting team efforts and assuming responsibilities to help when asked. In other words, it is their job to widen span of support for these positions and units.

## LEVER 4: SHARED RESPONSIBILITIES

The discussion in previous chapters has focused largely on the rights accorded to individuals: the rights to control resources, set goals, make decisions, and influence the work of others. In fact, our definition of organization design—the system of accountability that defines key positions in an organization and legitimates the rights of these positions—formalizes this perspective.

With rights, of course, come responsibilities. Some responsibilities are explicit—shaped by unit structure, diagnostic control systems, and interactive networks. These responsibilities are hardwired into the organization through formal design choices. Other responsibilities are implicit: they are not found in any organization chart but rather are embedded in informal norms and shared expectations.

This chapter focuses on the fourth design lever: shared responsibilities (figure 6-1). *Shared responsibilities* are the obligations that individuals assume to help others who are working toward shared goals. As with the other design levers—unit structure, diagnostic control systems, and interactive networks—managers must design and build these shared responsibilities to suit their organization and then ensure that they are widely embraced.

The purpose in designing shared responsibilities is to widen spans of support and increase people's commitment to others. To achieve this result, shared responsibilities typically focus on the following:

- Responsibility to customers

- Responsibility to the mission (e.g., a military unit)

- Responsibility to the team or individuals

- Responsibility to constituents

The ideal of shared responsibilities is exemplified by Johnson & Johnson's well-known credo, which was adopted in 1943. The credo is reproduced in figure 6-4.

The credo begins with responsibility to customers: "We believe our first *responsibility* is to the doctors, nurses and patients, to mothers and fathers and all others who use our products and services." Each subsequent paragraph begins with the words "We are *responsible*," affirming additional responsibilities to employees, communities, and stockholders (emphasis added).

In a similar vein, investment bank Goldman Sachs issues wallet cards to all employees stating the firm's long-standing core values related to shared responsibilities: client first, team second, and individual last. As a Goldman partner stated, "We have had years of training in putting the team ahead of the individual."[6]

Remembering that the goal of using this design lever is to widen span of support, shared responsibilities should reflect ideals that transcend self-interest and financial returns. Extolling wealth creation for shareholders is rarely sufficient to motivate people to help others. But it is important to recognize that Johnson & Johnson—like other high-performing companies—does not choose mission at the expense of performance. The last line of its credo reads, "When we operate according to these principles, the stockholders should realize a fair return."

FIGURE 6-4

### Johnson & Johnson's Credo

We believe our first responsibility is to the doctors, nurses and patients, to mothers and fathers and all others who use our products and services. In meeting their needs everything we do must be of high quality. We must constantly strive to reduce our costs in order to maintain reasonable prices. Customers' orders must be serviced promptly and accurately. Our suppliers and distributors must have an opportunity to make a fair profit.

We are responsible to our employees, the men and women who work with us throughout the world. Everyone must be considered as an individual. We must respect their dignity and recognize their merit. They must have a sense of security in their jobs. Compensation must be fair and adequate, and working conditions clean, orderly and safe. We must be mindful of ways to help our employees fulfill their family responsibilities. Employees must feel free to make suggestions and complaints. There must be equal opportunity for employment, development and advancement for those qualified. We must provide competent management, and their actions must be just and ethical.

We are responsible to the communities in which we live and work and to the world community as well. We must be good citizens—support good works and charities and bear our fair share of taxes. We must encourage civic improvements and better health and education. We must maintain in good order the property we are privileged to use, protecting the environment and natural resources.

Our final responsibility is to our stockholders. Business must make a sound profit. We must experiment with new ideas. Research must be carried on, innovative programs developed and mistakes paid for. New equipment must be purchased, new facilities provided and new products launched. Reserves must be created to provide for adverse times. When we operate according to these principles, the stockholders should realize a fair return.

*Source:* Reprinted from Johnson & Johnson's 2004 annual report.

Based on its strong foundation of shared responsibility—and the commitment to others that it engenders—Johnson & Johnson has dominated its competitors both in its product markets and in financial performance for decades, and it is consistently ranked as one of America's most admired corporations.[7]

The critical issue, of course, is how managers can transform individual responsibility to shared responsibility. Research in social psychology suggests that four variables are important in creating a widely embraced sense of shared responsibility in any organization:

- Shared purpose

- Group identification

- Trust

- Equity

## Shared Purpose

One of the enduring lessons from psychological research over the past decades is the importance of *shared purpose* in creating shared responsibilities. People who are committed to a common purpose form cohesive groups that pull together and avoid the inevitable parochialism that fragments individuals and sub-groups in different directions.

More than forty years ago, researchers demonstrated that subgroups that initially distrusted and disliked each other became willing to cooperate and interact productively when leaders successfully established broad, overarching goals.[8] More recently, popular writers have made the same point by focusing on the importance of purpose in organizations (e.g., *Built to Last*) and in everyday life (e.g., *The Purpose-Driven Life*). As one manager stated, "It's fine to emphasize what we must shoot for, but we also must know what we stand for."[9]

Sometimes purpose is embedded in mission, which becomes the shared goal. Mintzberg explains with the following example:

> The mission of the hamburger franchise is to feed its clients, its goal perhaps to make money (or friends, or whatever). If the owner could make more money selling fanbelts, he probably would. In contrast, the gourmet chef who runs his own restaurant prepares the meals to satisfy himself as well as his clients; he would no sooner sell fanbelts than hamburgers. In other words, both organizations pursue the same

mission, but only in the second one is that mission also a goal—an end as well as a means. The primary goal of the gourmet restaurant is to perform its mission well.[10]

When the sense of shared purpose and mission is strong— whether it is preparing restaurant meals, offering community services, or coordinating battle plans—people throughout the organization are more likely to feel committed to helping each other. Achieving the mission becomes a shared responsibility.

In nonprofit organizations, which typically cannot afford to pay market-based wages, the creation of mission-driven commitment is essential to attract talented and skilled individuals. But similar situations can be found in any business. One of the reasons for Starbucks' phenomenal growth was management's ability to make employees, most of whom receive relatively low wages, feel committed to its mission and part of a family with a shared purpose and shared responsibilities.[11]

### Group Identification

All of us identify to varying degrees with the groups to which we belong—sports teams, schools, a department or function, or a business. In fact, the prestige and affiliation created by group membership help us understand who we are—our concept of self.[12]

Of course, different groups have different goals and subcultures. Even within the same organization, individuals must choose subgroup affiliations. The director of finance may choose to identify primarily with her functional specialty (finance), the business unit to which she is attached (a product unit), or the overall corporation. These choices are called *nested social dilemmas*. Each individual must decide whether to satisfy self-interest, the interests of the subgroup to which he or she belongs, or the interests of the overall organization.[13]

Because individuals are more likely to help those who are part of groups with which they identify, it is important that people identify strongly with those who are working toward the same purpose.[14] Commitment to a particular group guides an individual's actions when presented with choices that must be decided in favor of one group or another. Thus, the propensity to help others—or to accept help from others—is influenced strongly by the level of group identification, the similarity of members within the group, and the level of competition between subgroups.[15]

To build such identification, managers at Commerce Bank, an innovative bank delivering high levels of service to retail depositors, created an environment where employees felt part of an elite and exclusive cadre. Each new employee was given a set of cards that invited an individual to apply for a job at Commerce. Employees were encouraged to hand out these cards to anyone who provided them with exceptional service in their day-to-day life. To promote a feeling of distinctiveness, the company made it well known to employees that thousands of resumes were reviewed for a small number of positions when it entered a new metropolitan market. These practices, combined with a strong commitment to "wowing" customers, instilled strong feelings of exclusivity and group identification in the workforce.[16]

General Motors has both benefited and suffered from the power of subgroup identification. To foster creativity and learning, GM set up its Saturn division away from corporate headquarters in Detroit. As a result, new and important ideas were developed at Saturn. By the same token, however, strong identification with automobile subgroups created resistance to helping other groups:

I worked for General Motors but I worked for Pontiac, and my identity was ten times stronger around Pontiac than it was General Motors. . . . So I think the very thing that was our perceived strength at this point in time started to eat you alive. Because we'd get this very proud group of people, and then somebody comes in from outside and says, "I come from the [particular division] and we do great stuff." We are probably more receptive to somebody that comes in from the outside that we hire and shares ideas with us than somebody who comes in from another unit with GM to share ideas.[17]

In some circumstances, group identification may be constrained by design. Procter & Gamble, for example, produces both Tide and Cheer detergents. But consumers are loyal to the brand—either Tide or Cheer—and not to Procter & Gamble. Accordingly, inside Procter & Gamble, separate marketing units are set up to compete for scarce resources. Commitment to helping others is limited, by design, to the brand units to which individuals belong.

To foster group identification and a sense of shared responsibilities, managers often work hard to ensure that employees feel part of a family, offering each other mutual support and assistance when needed. In a series of interviews at Southwest Airlines, for example, family was the word used most often by employees to describe their work life experience.[18] Similarly, the dramatic success of a large health care company's diabetes disease management program in Hawaii—a model for the rest of the organization—was attributed to close teamwork among physicians, medical assistants, nurses, and administrators who operate in a culture best described by the Hawaiian word "Ohana," which translates to *family* in English.[19]

## Trust

For shared responsibilities to take hold, trust is essential. Social psychologists define *trust* as a willingness to be vulnerable to the actions of another based on the expectation that the other party will perform a desired action in the absence of monitoring or control.[20] Trust is necessary when goals cannot be achieved alone and individuals are exposed to risk as a result of their requests for help.[21] Individuals must not fear exploitation if they ask for assistance or respond to requests for help from other individuals or subgroups.

When trust is present, individuals can have confidence that stepping forward to offer help to other group members will be reciprocated in the future. Moreover, trust often creates important norms of shared responsibilities even when no direct future exchange or reciprocity is anticipated.[22]

When the need for trust is high—notably in organizations where shared responsibility is an important design lever—many organizations promote only from within. This policy is necessary to ensure that senior managers have rotated through many different positions and have demonstrated a long-standing commitment to shared organizational goals and a commitment to others. For this reason, a promote-from-within policy is the norm at Johnson & Johnson and at other companies that emphasize shared responsibility as a core value.

It's not hard to find examples of the effects of a lack of trust. Researchers have shown, for example, that business students from a university that emphasized teamwork and cooperation were reluctant to enter into a cooperative game with students from a nearby business school. The reputation of the second school for exploitive and uncooperative behavior sabotaged the potential cooperation between the two groups.[23] Similar results have been found for groups belonging to the same overall organization, such as separate units within the same firm.

Trust, of course, can be highly idiosyncratic. Within an organization, an individual may trust one person but not another. Thus, as with influence networks, you could also analytically map out trust networks—in this case indicating who trusted whom.[24]

Unfortunately, trust can be destroyed quickly in any organization. Layoffs in economic downturns pose particular problems. When downsizing cannot be avoided, managers of organizations that rely on wide spans of support invest considerable resources in employee communication, benefit packages, and placement assistance to ensure that all concerned feel fairly treated in the circumstances.[25]

## Equity

Much of the work in previous chapters has focused on structures and systems to promote efficiency and effectiveness. For the most part, the discussions have ignored *equity*—the fairness of the distribution of resources and rewards among those who contribute to the organization's success. However, when wide spans of support are required, equity issues become critically important.

The concept is straightforward: regardless of favorable psychological conditions—common purpose, group identification, and trust—individuals will not step forward to help others achieve shared goals if they perceive that the fruits of their efforts will be expropriated unfairly or shared inequitably. Inequity breeds resentment. And if individuals resent the rewards or resources that others are receiving, they will resist helping them. Thus, if wide spans of support are important for effective organizational functioning, managers must ensure that individuals who are asked to assume responsibility for helping others feel that the rewards of their efforts are shared fairly.

The importance of equitable pay was illustrated in the cost savings realized by a steel manufacturer that implemented a new activity-based costing system. With the introduction of the new system, many long-standing products and customers were shown to be unprofitable. In normal circumstances, it would have been extremely difficult to raise prices or abandon unprofitable products because of the resulting reduction in sales commissions. In this case, however, managers were able to raise prices and turn down unprofitable accounts. Salespeople were willing to help reposition the business because they were compensated by salary and because managers promised that cost savings would be shared widely and equitably across the company.[26]

Compensation is the most obvious example of the importance of equity to shared responsibilities, but titles (or any other trappings of authority that make individuals feel inferior) can create potential impediments to a willingness to assume responsibility to help other people. For this reason, the legendary Thomas J. Watson Sr.—who built IBM to greatness during his thirty years as CEO—required all employees to remove titles and ranks from their office doors and desk placards and eliminated reserved parking spaces for executives. He also abandoned piecework compensation in all IBM factories because he believed the practice devalued the status of workers.[27]

## THE IMPORTANCE OF LEADERSHIP

To summarize: when managers want to create an ethos of shared responsibilities, they must first engender a sense of shared purpose so that people can feel pride in participating in the mission of the organization. Second, they must build a cohesive group to which people want to belong and identify. Third, managers must instill norms of integrity and trust so that people believe that commitments will be honored. Finally, managers must ensure that all who participate in creating value—especially those who reach out to help others—feel that the distribution of rewards is fair and just.

All of these ingredients are necessary to create shared responsibilities to others. But they are not sufficient. To ensure that people throughout the organization embrace shared responsibilities, leaders must lead the way. To create an environment of trust and support, leaders must themselves exemplify the ideals to which they ask the broader organization to commit.[28] As a result, slips in integrity—no matter how small—are generally sufficient to disqualify managers from leadership positions.

More generally, if leaders want people to reach out and help others, they must do the same. Leaders must act as role models; in popular jargon, they must walk the talk. To signal the importance of responsibility to others, Herb Kelleher, CEO of Southwest Airlines, routinely helps out when he is traveling—logging in passengers or helping clean the aircraft after passengers have deplaned.

Of course, putting the right people in key positions is critical if senior managers want to ensure that norms of shared responsibility permeate the organization. Therefore, leaders must select and promote only those who have demonstrated the capacity to assume responsibility for helping others achieve shared goals. To ensure that the right people are identified, promotion is generally from within: it takes a long time to inculcate desired values and evaluate people's capability to assume shared responsibilities relating to customers, mission, and teamwork.

This means that leaders must hold subordinates accountable not only for achieving specific goals but also for their personal behavior. Because commitment to shared responsibility cannot be measured, such evaluation must be subjective. This does not mean, however, that accountability for commitment is soft and unenforceable. In fact, it is the hardest accountability of all: those who exemplify a high level of commitment to help others and to assume shared responsibilities are promoted and asked to assume important leadership positions. Those who fail to respond when asked to help a customer, or those who are unwilling to assist other units in achieving shared goals, are disqualified for consideration for senior leadership positions.

This is a difficult test. Many would argue that organizations should be designed to reflect the strengths and weaknesses of the available people. In other words, the organization design should be tailored to fit the complement of existing skills.[29] But when spans of support must be wide, specific character traits cannot be negotiable: for these organizations, senior managers must find, train, and develop only individuals of high personal integrity who embrace shared responsibilities and can deliver on a commitment to help others.

For this reason, family business networks—even in multibillion-dollar enterprises—are the mainstay of all emerging economies. The allegiance of family members is clear. They can be trusted to accept shared responsibilities and to protect the interests of the family business. In Western economies, accountability can be enforced relatively easily through regulations, governance structures, and a highly developed legal system. In emerging economies, these institutions are too weak to be reliable. Only family members can be counted on to honor responsibilities that might otherwise be unenforceable.[30]

Many successful businesses have adopted this concept by making employees feel that they are an integral part of an extended and caring "business family," with the understanding that acceptance into the family confers an obligation to support shared responsibilities.

## SHARED RESPONSIBILITIES AND STRATEGY

It is important to understand that commitment to others and shared responsibilities, although noble traits, are not ends in themselves. Like the other levers, they are a means to an end: the effective implementation of strategy. For some strategies, commitment to others is not critical to success, and spans of support can be narrow. In these cases, managers can avoid the substantial investments in time, attention, and resources needed to build widely shared responsibilities. For other strategies, however, there is no choice except to widen spans of support.

For example, consider Southwest Airlines, a low-cost airline founded in 1971 to serve the regional markets of Texas.[31] Over time, Southwest's no-frills, low-price value proposition found favor with customers. It successfully expanded around the country, setting up operations close to major cities in out-of-the-way, second-tier airports that the major carriers had avoided.

The overarching goal was clear: to beat the major carriers. To keep asset utilization high and costs low, Southwest standardized its fleet of fuel-efficient 737 aircraft and worked hard to keep its planes in the air as much as possible. Southwest had the best on-time performance, fewest lost bags, and lowest level of customer complaints in the airline industry. Minimizing time on the ground to ensure on-time departures was a key ingredient of its strategy. Aircraft were routinely turned around at the gate in less than fifteen minutes even though Southwest used fewer than half the personnel used by the major carriers; this process included disembarking inbound passengers, cleaning and fueling the aircraft, boarding outbound passengers, and pushing back from the gate.

For this strategy to succeed, commitment to helping others was extremely important. All employees had to pitch in—no matter what their job descriptions—to get the plane ready for takeoff as quickly as possible. It was common to find flight attendants and pilots helping clean the aircraft and checking in passengers to ensure on-time departures. Although Southwest offered no in-flight amenities, customer loyalty was still high. Not only were prices low, but employees consistently offered warm and friendly service—often hosting impromptu skits and other enjoyable in-flight events. (The word *customer* was always capitalized in corporate communications, and employees routinely volunteered to help customers in need.)

None of this would have been possible without the right kind of people. Accordingly, Southwest managers placed a great deal of emphasis on finding and hiring individuals with positive attitudes who valued teamwork. Most new employees were willing to take a pay cut to join the company. Managers worked hard to cultivate a feeling of distinctiveness: employees were made to feel part of a special family in which management was interested in each person as an individual. Hiring was very selective. Only 3 percent of applicants were offered positions. Front-line employees interviewed all prospective job candidates before they were considered by the hiring office. To avoid importing bad attitudes and work-to-rule procedures from other airlines, preference was given to applicants who did not have airline experience. If employees felt that an applicant would not be a good fit for the company, the candidate was removed from further consideration.

Management and employees were constantly sharing information and ideas; the themes heard most often were customer service, family, equality, cost consciousness, dedication, and fun. Employees were empowered to make local decisions without management approval and oversight. Compensation was egalitarian: pay across positions was relatively flat, with differences based on seniority and not individual performance. Stock options were awarded widely so that all employees felt like owners.

CEO Herb Kelleher—who was proud of the fact that he was named one of the five lowest-paid CEOs in Dallas—was famous inside the company for walking the talk. Kelleher pitched in to help gate crews every time he traveled, spent a great deal of time talking with customers and individual employees at all ranks, routinely sent notes and birthday cards, participated in a wide range of company events, and paid special attention to ensuring that the right people were hired and promoted for key positions. As a union leader stated, "How many CEOs do you know who come into a cleaner's break room at 3 a.m. on a Sunday passing out doughnuts or putting on a pair of overalls to clean a plane?"[32]

At Southwest Airlines, the sense of shared responsibility was very strong. The strategy appeared to be working. By 2004, Southwest's market capitalization was greater than that of all other U.S. airlines combined.[33]

## Overcoming Resistance

As with the other levers of organization design, attempts to widen span of support through shared responsibilities can be met by resistance. Managers must avoid three pitfalls in particular:

- The perils of pay

- The zero-sum game

- The blame game

### The Perils of Pay

If managers decide that commitment to others is not necessary to successfully implement strategy, they can (and probably should) mirror a market-based system and reward only individual performance. Tournaments—internal competitions using a winner-take-all strategy—can be used to motivate individuals to strive for promotions and financial rewards. Star performers can be paid disproportionately more than others, and everyone in the organization can be made aware of the differential.

If strategy requires wide spans of support, however, the power of individualized incentives can be destructive. As a result, in mission-based organizations (e.g., religious orders, universities, and the military), pay scales are always based on seniority and rank, with little account of individual merit or performance. This also is true in business organizations that require exceptional effort from employees based on team commitment to mission. At Southwest Airlines, as noted earlier, employees are not paid according to performance but rather according to a predetermined schedule based on seniority.

Team-based rewards typically include some aspect of gain-sharing based on team output or overall corporate performance. Often, employees participate in profit sharing, stock purchase, and, for some, stock option plans. At the limit, everyone is paid by salary, and bonus compensation is based on overall corporate performance as a percentage of base pay. (In such situations, of course, managers must ensure that "free riders" do not jeopardize perceived equity.)

When pay is team-based, the compensation of high-potential people will likely be lower than the amount they could earn pursuing other opportunities. This problem is extreme in nonprofit organizations, where typical pay is substantially below competitive market levels. Not surprisingly, these organizations rely heavily on commitment to mission and the positive effects of contribution and group affiliation as "psychic income."[34]

Even when managers choose to retain individual performance evaluation, a significant portion of an individual's evaluation will still focus on team building and team support skills. In such circumstances, companies often elicit feedback from a 360-degree evaluation process that asks superiors, subordinates, and peers (both inside the unit and from other units) to comment on the willingness of the individual to contribute to shared goals and support the work of others.

At the top of the organization, executive compensation can be an explosive issue if workers and lower-level managers feel that senior executives are expropriating an unfair share of corporate profits. The fact that average CEO compensation in 2000 was more than five hundred times as much as the amount paid to the lowest-ranked workers is not a recipe for creating wide spans of support.[35] To avoid such feelings of inequity,

Costco CEO James Sinegal publicly capped his salary and bonus at twice the level of a Costco store manager.[36] At least in part as a result, losses from employee theft at Costco are less than one-tenth the levels experienced by other retail companies.[37]

Going one step further, some senior executives share their bonus compensation with subordinates to reinforce the importance of shared responsibilities. In support of a new "on-demand" customer strategy that required complex integration among software, hardware, services, and consulting, IBM CEO Sam Palmisano turned over a portion of his annual bonus to be shared among other IBM senior managers.[38] Similarly, during the market downturn in financial services, John Mack, CEO of Credit Suisse First Boston, gave up $20 million of his bonus and persuaded hundreds of others in his firm to do the same. As he stated, "It's about fairness and building a great firm."[39]

## The Zero-Sum Game

In organizations where managers create a culture of winners and losers, resistance to assuming shared responsibilities is inevitable. Performance evaluation systems in which managers periodically rank the performance of employees and then discharge those who fall in the bottom of the range have the potential to set up this problem. General Electric pioneered this approach and used it to routinely identify and discharge the bottom 5 percent of its workforce. At Harvard Business School, instructors are required to rank all students in each course and award those in the bottom 10 percent a "Category III" grade (students who receive an excessive number of these grades are then subject to academic review). Such systems generally provide a healthy discipline, but, if abused, they can create fear and reluctance to help others. At Enron, this "rank-and-yank" system was taken to the extreme, with the bottom 20 percent being subject to dismissal each year.

In a chapter titled "When Internal Competition Turns Friends into Enemies," Pfeffer and Sutton discuss how internal competition at Microsoft hurt teamwork, resulting in the release of bug-prone software.[40] Bonuses at Microsoft were based on a forced-curve zero-sum ranking. There was no incentive—in fact, there was a disincentive—to help anyone else do their job more effectively. As a result, workers spent excessive energy in hiding problems to avoid blame instead of fixing the problems to ensure a high-quality product.

Based on their analysis, Pfeffer and Sutton summarize five practices that undermine cooperative behavior:

- Forced rankings that limit the number of people who can receive the highest evaluation

- Individual recognition awards, such as employee of the month

- Forced distributions of merit raise pools

- Contests between units or individuals for monetary and nonmonetary prizes

- Published rankings of unit and individual performance

Of course, as discussed in previous chapters, these same practices can also be powerful motivators of individual achievement. Thus, to determine whether or not to adopt specific practices, managers must analyze the importance of wide spans of support to the successful implementation of their strategy and then design performance measurement systems to narrow or widen spans of support accordingly.

## The Blame Game

The final source of resistance to assuming responsibility to help others is a culture in which senior managers are quick to find culprits to blame for failures. Some managers take pride in their ability to inject fear of the consequences of poor performance. Such a shoot-the-messenger environment makes it dangerous for individuals to stick their necks out to become associated with any activities outside their span of control and accountability.

Again, the actions of senior executives as role models are critical. If senior executives are constantly criticizing each other or creating a culture of ridicule and blame, employees in these units are unlikely to take seriously any responsibility to step outside their units to help others. Span of support will be narrow. Ford Motor Company, notorious for interdivisional rivalries, experienced this problem. Even as the company celebrated its centennial anniversary in 2003, CEO William Clay Ford Jr. found it difficult to achieve teamwork and a shared focus on restoring the business to profitability.[41]

When spans of support must be wide—to support interactive networks, build customer loyalty, or sustain a complex value chain—skilled executives sometimes take unusual steps to counteract any potential for a blame culture. As one observer explained:

> I was impressed, some years ago, by a counterintuitive method devised by a manager at Intel. Every quarter, he threw a big dinner—not for the group that had been most successful, but for "the failure of the month." The celebration honored the group that had made a valiant effort that just didn't pan out. Failures, that manager wanted his people to know, were an inevitable accompaniment of risk taking. They should be talked about openly, not hidden, papered over, or blamed on others.[42]

Such an effort may seem unusual, but it is essential in any organization where responsibility to others is critical for the implementation of a long-term sustainable strategy.

Human nature is a key organization design variable.

- A critical task of senior managers is to decide how they wish individuals to act in their organizations and then create the necessary conditions for them to act in the desired ways.

- *Definition:* Span of support defines the range of support that an individual can anticipate and expect from people in other organizational units.

- Commitment to others is important for
  - Strategies based on customer loyalty
  - Organizations that have complex designs

- *Definition:* Shared responsibilities are the obligations that individuals assume to help others who are working toward shared goals.

- To create shared responsibilities, leadership is paramount.

- Requirements for assuming responsibilities to help others working toward shared goals include
  - Shared purpose
  - Group identification
  - Trust
  - Equity

- People will resist helping others when they perceive that they are competing in a zero-sum game for rewards or promotion, when pay is inequitable, or when failures or risk-taking are punished.

## ACTION STEPS

**FIGURE 6-5**

**Lever 4: Shared Responsibilities**

1. Assess the importance of customer loyalty to your strategy and the complexity of your organization's design.

2. Determine the necessary level of commitment to others and the appropriate span of support for different units and positions.

3. Establish shared responsibilities by

   • Articulating and visibly committing to shared purpose and mission

   • Creating group pride and identification through selection, training, and team recognition

   • Ensuring that the distribution of rewards is perceived to be fair and equitable

   • Promoting only those individuals who demonstrate responsibility for mission success and helping others

4. Lead the way: be trustworthy and act with integrity.

# 7

---

# ADJUSTING THE LEVERS:
# THREE EXAMPLES

YOU NOW HAVE STUDIED the four levers of organization design: unit structure, diagnostic control systems, interactive networks, and shared responsibilities. To this point, the book has presented examples to illustrate specific techniques. In this chapter, the analysis highlights the importance of the interplay of each design variable on the others. For the first time, you'll look at examples of how the levers can be integrated and used together.

We focus on three organizations: two commercial and one nonprofit. Each description is a snapshot of an organization at a different point in time. The first organization is chosen because of its successful use of matrix accountability. The second firm shows how to balance responsiveness to customers with economies of scale and technical excellence. The third organization reveals how these principles work in a nonprofit setting.

The names of all three organizations have been disguised. They represent different industries, different parts of the world,

and different time periods. But the lessons that you can draw
from them are important and enduring.

## EXAMPLE 1: MATRIX REDUX

In chapter 5, I stated that implementing a matrix successfully is
the acid test of organization design. This most demanding of all
organizational forms *can* work, but implementing a matrix is not
for the faint of heart. *All* the levers of organization design must
be carefully adjusted and functioning properly.

It's easy to understand the desire to implement a matrix organization. Driven by advancing technology, markets have become global, product technologies more sophisticated, and
customers more knowledgeable and demanding. As a result,
managers must wrestle with how to offer superior products at
low prices tailored to individual customer needs.

As argued in chapter 3, choosing a structural configuration
allows an organization to focus scarce resources on delivering
low cost, regional customization, or product excellence. But
using a pure configuration to focus attention on one dimension
of strategy reduces the attention that can be focused on other dimensions. Many managers are uncomfortable with this choice.
They feel that their organization needs to do more than one
thing exceptionally well: it must simultaneously deliver advanced technology, offer low prices, and maintain a focus on
local markets. One-dimensional approaches, they argue, are un-
acceptable in competitive global markets.

A matrix design solves this dilemma by simultaneously focusing an organization on multiple dimensions of value creation. Using a matrix design, managers can have their cake and
eat it too. A matrix structure has two or more equally weighted
sets of unit groupings: one group structured by product line, for
example, and a second group structured by geographic region.
As a result, unit heads in a matrix organization are accountable

to two bosses—in this example, one boss who is interested in regional performance and another who is concerned with product line performance.

Notwithstanding its intended advantages, the matrix design has had a checkered history. During the 1970s, matrix organizations were all the rage. Academics and consultants trumpeted their virtues. By the 1980s, however, matrix organizations had fallen out of favor: managers found them to be unworkable. The problems inherent in matrix organizations were predictable and predicted. In 1978, Davis and Lawrence anticipated what would ultimately cause the downfall of many attempts to implement matrix forms of organization:

- Confusion about priorities when employees are accountable to more than one boss

- Internal power struggles for resources

- Time wasted in group decision making

- High overhead costs due to redundancies

- Excessive internal focus drawing attention away from external markets

- Too much democracy and too little action[1]

Today, the matrix has resurfaced, but the jury is still out: can these organizations work? If so, under what circumstances? The following section describes how top management at Alpha Co. (a disguised name) adjusted the levers of organization design to counter the problems inherent in any matrix design.

## Alpha Co.

Alpha was a diversified manufacturing company with worldwide operations in more than one hundred forty countries. Its engineered products included transportation (e.g., rail cars), power plants (e.g., hydro and nuclear), environmental and process controls, and robotics. With more than two hundred thousand employees, Alpha generated more than $30 billion in revenue.

Because Alpha's product markets spanned a wide range of technology-based equipment, it was critical for the company to be at the forefront of technological innovation and to exploit economies of scale in R&D and production. Customers, no matter where they were located in the world, wanted the latest and best functionality and technology.

Rail systems, hydroelectric generation equipment, and power substations typically were purchased by governments or government-supported corporations. Accordingly, political considerations also played an important role in purchasing decisions. In evaluating bids, customers required suppliers such as Alpha to respond to local political sensitivities by hiring local labor, sourcing local materials whenever possible, and having a stand-alone subsidiary domiciled in their country to comply with local regulations and pay tax on local profits.

To respond to this unique competitive environment, Alpha's CEO decided that the company must be both global (to capture the best of global product technology) and local (to respond to national governments); be both big (to drive economies of scale in production and technology) and small (to be agile and fast moving); and be radically decentralized (to foster innovation and entrepreneurial spirit) but with centralized reporting and control (to ensure accountability for the consistent implementation of strategy).

A matrix design was the organizational vehicle chosen to balance these tensions.

### Dual Accountability

Because Alpha's typical customers were nationally based purchasers of industrial equipment, one design alternative would be to organize Alpha Co. using the local value creation configuration. In this configuration, separate market-facing units are created in each country, each with full manufacturing and distribution capabilities. Span of control for market-facing managers is set very wide to ensure that they have the resources needed to respond to the unique needs of their local customers.

But the nature of Alpha's technology-based products complicated this prescription. World-class technology—leveraging both R&D and manufacturing on a global basis—was essential. The company could not afford the duplication and redundancy that pure regionalization would have created. Alternatively, Alpha could have organized using the global standard of excellence configuration. In this archetype, powerful centralized operating core units such as R&D and manufacturing are given wide spans of control and are responsible for rationalizing global resources and leveraging best practices.

Alpha's top managers wanted to be both global and local. To balance these inherent tensions, they chose a specific matrix design: managers would create units for each region (to respond to the needs of national customers) and for each major product category (to leverage scale in technology, production, and sourcing and distribution).

Figure 7-1 illustrates Alpha's matrix concept.

On the regional dimension of the matrix, thirteen hundred separate legal entities were created to operate in one hundred forty countries. These market-facing units were responsible for staying close to customers, maintaining relationships with local governments, and ensuring local labor and material content. On the product dimension, more than sixty-five product groups were combined into seven business segments. These centrally managed operating-core units were responsible for global product strategies, worldwide technology, and global sourcing and production to create economies of scale.

Thus, each manager at Alpha was expected to focus on two dimensions simultaneously: region and product. As a result,

**FIGURE 7-1**

## Alpha Co. Matrix Reporting Relationships

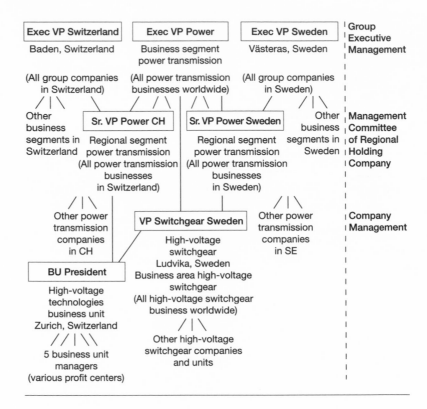

each unit manager had two bosses. Referring to figure 7-1, a manager of a business unit described how it all worked:

> My company is part of the power transmission business here in Switzerland. Going up the regional part of the matrix, I report directly to one boss, who is responsible for all of the various power transmission businesses based in Switzerland. He in turn reports to an executive vice president, who is responsible for all Alpha businesses—power transmission and others—in Switzerland.
>
> On the product dimension, I report directly to a second boss, who sits in Sweden. He is responsible for businesses

like mine—high-voltage switchgear—all around the world. He reports to the executive vice president in charge of the power transmission segment of the business worldwide.

Thus, I am directly responsible to two bosses. I have to coordinate my strategies and targets with each of them, be prepared to answer their individual concerns, and be accountable to both for my performance.

But each of them also answers to two masters. My regional boss reports to the regional manager responsible for Switzerland and to the business segment manager responsible for power transmission worldwide. Similarly, my product line boss, who sits in Sweden and runs the Swedish switchgear company, reports to a regional segment manager responsible for all transmission businesses in Sweden and to the head of the worldwide power transmission segment.

### IT-Based Performance Measurement

Given the complexity of Alpha's strategy and its complex matrix structure, it was essential to have diagnostic control systems capable of supporting dual accountability. To respond to the demand to be both big and small, Alpha businesses around the world were divided into forty-five hundred profit centers. Although a typical profit center comprised only fifty people, spans of accountability were very wide. Managers of each profit center were responsible for overall business results: revenue growth, gross margin, and profit on the profit wheel; operating cash, receivables, and inventory on the cash wheel; and return on equity.

At first glance, it appears that the wide spans of accountability were well aligned with wide spans of control: each of the forty-five hundred profit centers controlled its own assets and had its own balance sheet and income statement, and business unit managers were accountable for measures that they controlled. But control of resources was not this straightforward.

Every resource—whether people, a factory, or a distribution network—was controlled simultaneously by two managers, each having different goals and agendas.

As a result, global product targets constantly had to be reconciled with regional targets for each business unit. To ensure that the matrix did not provide an excuse for delay and inaction, accountability encompassed not only specific financial performance measures but also accountability for action. To this end, the CEO promoted a "7-3 formula," which stipulated that it was better to decide quickly and be right only seven out of ten times rather than procrastinate to wait for the perfect solution. As he stated, "The only thing that we cannot accept is people who do nothing."

Alpha's success in implementing the matrix was enabled in large part by advances in information technology. A centralized data warehouse reporting system called ABACUS provided accurate and timely information on worldwide sales, orders, margins, and expenses. Each decentralized reporting unit (i.e., the forty-five hundred profit centers) entered standardized accounting information at its local site. After consolidation, this information was uploaded by satellite to headquarters and entered into a hierarchical database. Managers anywhere in the company could then download information from the database and parse it to gain an understanding of the various performance dimensions of any business or region.

Using ABACUS, diagnostic control systems could be configured to quickly and easily report performance information simultaneously to both country managers and product managers. To ensure that worldwide product managers were not at an informational disadvantage relative to country managers (who controlled the legal entities and therefore had ready access to local performance indicators), internal operating rules stipulated that only data from ABACUS could be used for performance monitoring and control. No other reports were to be used to set accountabilities. Moreover, no information could be released from ABACUS to any manager early or in advance of general release. A manager explained:

> The matrix structure in such a large group would have been absolutely impossible ten or fifteen years ago because we did not have the ability to create information databases to support the two levels of oversight.
>
> The database allows us to cut the data any way we want: we can extract performance indicators by company, by region, and by worldwide product line. Every month, the data are compiled and issued simultaneously in a variety of different ways for managers with different responsibilities.
>
> The database is used most heavily by Business Segment and Business Area managers since this is the only way they can compile and access information about the units under their responsibility. Company managers always have legal entity reporting to fall back on.

To make this possible, all businesses were required to use the same chart of accounts and the same accounting definitions and procedures. As Alpha's controller explained, "The worst scenario is to have our CEO challenging managers based on data from our centralized accounting system and to have managers responding with local data that no one else has seen before."

### *Creating Tension*

The matrix structure and strong accountability system required large amounts of information to ensure coordination. Much of it came from ABACUS, but additional information—especially nonfinancial information—was also necessary. To achieve their goals, managers were forced to work intensively to

widen their spans of influence. Because each manager was receiving different targets from two bosses (regional and global
product), managers throughout the company were forced to negotiate conflicts and find ways of mobilizing resources to meet
the demands of conflicting objectives. Accordingly, an important part of every manager's job evaluation was the extent to
which he was able to figure out how to influence others to ensure a successful conclusion.

Top-down performance targets were set at a demanding
level, and budget commitments were never changed. As a manager explained, "Explanations for shortfall are never accepted.
Rather than listening to explanations, the discussion always focuses on what the manager will do to get back on track." Typically, solutions to performance problems necessitated working
closely with managers in multiple units.

As discussed in chapter 5, cost allocation systems and transfer-pricing policies can be used to widen spans of influence. At
Alpha, cost allocation was taken to an extreme: all direct and indirect costs, including central administration, engineering, and
applied R&D, were allocated down to individual products and
business units. In addition, each profit center was charged interest based on a cost of capital calculation for balance sheet assets
employed. Depreciation expense was calculated using replacement cost asset values (resulting in a higher charge to income
compared with historical cost methods). Transfer-pricing policies mandated that all transfers between Alpha companies be
priced at market prices.

These accounting policies had two effects. First, after the allocation of all corporate overheads and the addition of interest
charges for the cost of capital employed, each business operated
on a very thin profit margin: there was little room for sloppy
pricing or lost manufacturing efficiency. Second, managers
cared deeply about the level of costs that were allocated to them

by operating-core units and other business units. As a result, managers analyzed cost drivers carefully, and they constantly challenged other units and operating-core managers to demonstrate that they were operating as efficiently and effectively as possible.

Top managers found other ways to use their diagnostic control systems to increase creative tension. To promote competitive pressure and ensure that managers were constantly looking outside their own units for new ideas, global product executives routinely sent out comparative data that allowed each business unit to benchmark its own performance relative to that of its peers (see figure 7-2). Upon receiving these charts, managers contacted their peers in higher-performing units to explore the reasons. As a senior executive stated, "I have found in the past that it is extremely effective to select several variables to measure each month and send out the comparative charts to all the managers whose operations are being compared. I don't even have to say anything. Those managers will fight like crazy not to be low man on the rating."

**FIGURE 7-2**

**Alpha Co. Comparative Data Sent to Unit Managers**

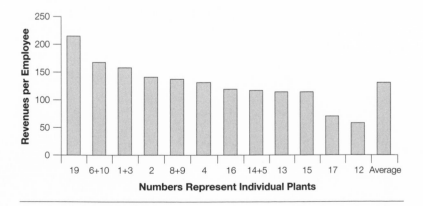

### *Three Strikes and You're Out*

Given the complexity of Alpha's strategy and structures, individuals had to be committed to helping others make the matrix work. In other words, spans of support had to be wide.

Putting the right type of people in key positions was critical for the successful implementation of Alpha's organization design. The CEO described the type of managers who would succeed in this demanding environment: people who were capable of leading others, generous with their support, and comfortable thinking in group terms. Individuals who did not possess these qualities would jeopardize the success of the matrix—and the success of the strategy.

To ensure that the right people held key management positions, the CEO enforced a very hard line for those who demonstrated a lack of responsibility for helping others. The rule was "three strikes and you're out": "If two managers cannot agree, escalate the issue up to your bosses for a decision. If you cannot agree a second time, go to your bosses again for a decision. But if you cannot agree a third time, both managers will be replaced."

Incentives were designed to facilitate wide spans of support. Compensation and bonuses reflected the importance of interaction and cross-unit coordination. For a typical profit center manager, 25 percent of the annual bonus was a function of shared worldwide business area product goals; 25 percent was allocated to personal goals, including commitment to the overall success of strategy implementation; and 50 percent was based on hitting targets for the manager's regional company.

### Adjusting the Levers to Support Alpha's Strategy

To make its complex matrix work, Alpha Co. had the engine of organization design firing on all cylinders. From a corporate vantage point, Alpha's four spans are illustrated in figure 7-3.

FIGURE 7-3

**Four Spans at Alpha Co.**

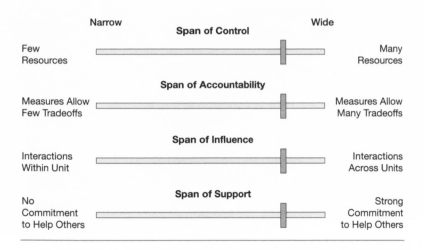

Managers at very low levels were given the full range of re-sources that they needed to achieve business results, and they were given the freedom to make tradeoffs about the use of those resources. Although the business was highly decentralized and had complex dual reporting relationships, managers at Alpha set out a clear structure; each manager knew precisely the resources he controlled and the performance variables for which he was accountable. Diagnostic control systems were configured to imple-ment strict accountability for financial performance throughout the business: all three wheels of financial accountability—profit, cash flow, and return on capital employed—were monitored carefully to ensure that each decentralized unit was making effi-cient use of its resources. Information technology was leveraged effectively using the ABACUS database system. In this way, managers were able to simultaneously extract performance data that responded to their span of accountability—whether by global product line or by region. Without ABACUS, the ac-countability necessary to support the structure would have been impossible.

Considerable creative tension was introduced into the business through stretch goals, the allocation of upstream overheads, and market-based transfer prices. Combined with the tensions of the two-dimensional matrix reporting structure, these tensions created wide-ranging interactive networks and wide spans of influence. To ensure adequate span of support, top managers were explicit about the importance of shared responsibilities. Those who were unable or unwilling to make ongoing commitments to help others achieve the overall business goals would be replaced. Responsibility to others was enforced by sanctions and threats of dismissal. An action orientation—decide and decide quickly—cascaded from the CEO down through the entire organization.

Could Alpha's matrix work with any of the four levers missing? Managers of many companies have tried to implement a matrix without carefully designing all four levers to compensate for the inherent problems of such a complex design. They have merely drawn the boxes of a matrix on their organization charts and hoped for the best. None have succeeded.

## EXAMPLE 2: RINGS AROUND THE CUSTOMER

Matrix organizations—with their dual solid line reporting relationships—represent the most radical attempt to group units simultaneously on two or more dimensions of business strategy. Because it is difficult to sustain a matrix organization, most firms attempt less demanding ways to balance responsiveness to customers with the needs of technology, regional focus, or industry expertise.

Beta, Inc.—another disguised company name—chose to organize by function to serve its customers. But, as you will see, Beta also uses the levers of organization design in unique ways to ensure that operating-core functions can develop superior technology and deliver excellent customer service.

## Beta, Inc.

Beta, Inc. was a fast-growing software development organization with more than eight thousand employees and $1 billion in sales. Beta's sophisticated business software products were sold to large corporate customers that were seeking global software solutions. Competition in Beta's market segment was fast moving and intense.

Because of the complexity of its products, two factors—successful installation and ongoing project support—were critical to customer satisfaction. Not only did Beta need to offer the latest technology, but it also had to be perceived as capable of delivering functional, trouble-free solutions in complex computing environments.

Top management at Beta believed that long-term customer satisfaction was the foremost driver of continuing success. Executives purchasing Beta, Inc.'s multimillion-dollar software often put their careers on the line by recommending Beta rather than competing products. Half of Beta's revenue came from repeat sales to existing customers. Accordingly, Beta's CEO was emphatic about the firm's focus:

> Our customers' success is the sole measure of our own success. And we will do whatever it takes to ensure that our customers succeed in their deployment and use of Beta applications. Doing whatever it takes means that when faced with conflicting priorities, we place our customers' interests above everything else. At Beta no consideration ever takes precedence over ensuring that our customers remain successful. Not new product development. Not marketing initiatives. Not new business. Satisfying our existing customers is our first priority.

For a typical customer, the actual purchase price of Beta's software was a small portion (typically 15 percent) of the total outlay. Most costs were expended on installation, system integration, and training. To capture this lucrative revenue stream, many of Beta's competitors had vertically integrated their businesses, offering customers not only software products but also consulting and system integration services. Beta followed a different path. Top managers decided that they would focus only on software development and sales; they would rely on third-party partners to supply the system integration, hardware, and training to ensure effective installation.

### Concentric Circles

Although Beta had more than eight thousand employees, it did not have a formal organization chart. In part, an organization chart was unnecessary because it was clear to everyone how the organization was designed: for the customer. In fact, Beta was designed in the dedicated service relationship configuration. However, managers envisioned their structure as a set of concentric rings built around the customer (see figure 7-4).

The first ring around the customer was the sales organization. As the principal market-facing unit, the sales organization was divided into five worldwide regions. Salespeople were dedicated to specific major customers and managed the customer relationship through the initial contact, specification of requirements, contract negotiations, installation, and assurance that the application was running smoothly.

Because of the technical complexity of the product, salespeople needed help from a variety of internal operating-core functions. The primary support group was product marketing—found in the second concentric circle around the customer—which provided product information and expertise. To ensure consistent quality around the world, product marketing was centralized at headquarters.

The product marketing function was divided into two subgroups, called *horizontals* and *verticals*. A horizontal subgroup

**FIGURE 7-4**

**Beta, Inc., Unit Structure**

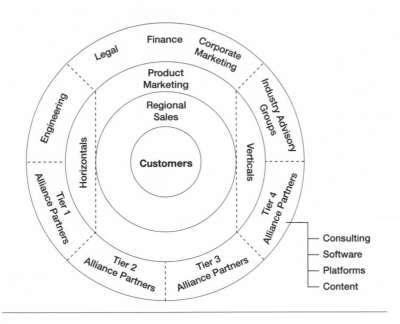

was created for each major product category. These groups, working closely with technical engineering, comprised product experts responsible for product planning, design, and positioning for each product category. The vertical subgroups, by contrast, were organized by industry. A separate vertical subgroup was created for each major industry segment (e.g., automotive, financial services, energy). Working closely with industry advisory boards, employees of the vertical subgroups customized standard Beta products to ensure that they were responsive to the unique needs of each subgroup's specific industry clients.

Product experts from the horizontal and the vertical subgroups accompanied salespeople during sales calls and assisted in the implementation of the project.

External alliance partners—independently owned firms and consulting practices—were located in the third concentric ring around the customer. More than seven hundred third-party partners provided the system integration, hardware, and expertise to install Beta's software and to ensure successful functioning for customers. Alliance partners were classified into tiers, depending on the importance of their ongoing relationship with Beta, and further classified into one of four service categories: consulting, software, platform, or content.

Other key groups supporting the customer sales effort—also located in the outermost ring—were corporate marketing (for customer referrals and selling support), professional services (for technical service support and product demonstrations), finance (to obtain pricing and discounts), and legal (for contract negotiation).

### Customer Satisfaction Is Money

Senior managers at Beta had identified several critical performance variables: financial performance, customer satisfaction, product quality, on-site implementation success, and relationships with alliance partners. Diagnostic control systems tracked all these variables. Cash flow was monitored carefully to ensure that the business stayed cash positive. In addition, managers tracked revenue, profit forecasts, and days of sales outstanding. These indicators were included in quarterly forecasts and were monitored closely by senior managers through weekly flash reports. To obtain accurate business forecasts, Beta used its own software (which was available as a product to its customers) to track customer orders and the prospective sales pipeline. This data provided an excellent window into future industry demand and allowed managers to scale the business up or down quickly in anticipation of industry growth or contraction.

Diagnostic control systems also tracked customer satisfaction and other nonfinancial measures. As one manager stated, "We measure customer satisfaction as if it were money." Customer satisfaction data was collected by an independent survey company to ensure objectivity and reliability. Using this data, every installation project was color-coded—green, yellow, or red—to indicate the amount of management attention needed to ensure successful product installation.

In addition to customer satisfaction, data was also collected on employee satisfaction, partner satisfaction, and product quality and defect rates. Managers believed that employee satisfaction was a leading indicator that would eventually lead to customer satisfaction and revenue growth. Alliance partner satisfaction was also measured and tracked carefully because external partners generated 75 percent of Beta's annual license revenues.

Information technology allowed the company to monitor critical performance variables at individual as well as unit levels. Quarterly performance reviews for all employees were managed through a companywide intranet. Achievements against targets and management's evaluation of each individual's performance were entered into the system regularly and tracked carefully.

Beta managers tightly aligned incentives with diagnostic control system measures. Bonuses, a large component of overall compensation, reflected achievements on key customer satisfaction targets. Bonuses were not fully paid when the sale agreement was signed and payment received. Instead, bonuses were held back until customer satisfaction data confirmed that the project was complete and the customer was fully satisfied.

In addition, Beta used a forced ranking system modeled on the system pioneered by General Electric. Every six months, employees in each unit were ranked on their performance and potential, and those falling in the bottom 5 percent were counseled out of the business. This system, called the Workforce Improvement Program, was intended to provide the discipline to separate low performers or those who were a poor fit with the culture of the organization.

Like Alpha's CEO, the CEO of Beta worked hard to create an action orientation. He told everyone in the business that it was better to decide quickly and act, even if the decision was right only 75 percent of the time. In his mind, delay was the enemy. As a result, meetings did not adjourn without a decision, and after a decision was made, all participants were expected to commit fully to its successful implementation.

### Transparent Goals

Everyone at Beta was accountable for customer satisfaction. Yet customer satisfaction depended on the work of many people in different departments and functions, as well as the performance of third-party alliance partners. No one person or department had all the resources necessary to satisfy a customer. As a result, managers had to figure out how to navigate complex webs of interdependencies to meet customer needs and ensure that emerging new products were on the forefront of technology.

One senior manager made this comment:

> To do my day-to-day job, I depend on sales, sales consulting, competency groups, alliances, technical support, corporate marketing, field marketing, and integrated marketing communications. None of these functions reports to me, and most do not even report to my group. Coordination happens because we all have customer satisfaction as our first priority. We are in constant communication, and we all are given consistent objectives.

As a result, span of accountability was invariably greater than span of control, creating an entrepreneurial gap and tension throughout the business. In addition, stretch goals, cascading from the top of the organization to the bottom and reinforced by the forced ranking system, continually signaled the importance of performance goals for everyone in the company. To get things done, managers and employees had to rely on interactive networks to expand their spans of influence. The fact that Beta had no organization chart allowed a broad interpretation of reporting relationships. As a result, it was acceptable to step outside unit boundaries.

Quarterly objectives for all employees—financial and non-financial—were posted on an intranet system and any employee could view them. Thus, if someone needed help for a new project or initiative, he or she could look up the objectives of any other person in the organization to ascertain where support could likely be found. Armed with knowledge about goals and accountabilities, individuals were empowered to influence others to ensure that their projects were adequately represented. The transparency and accessibility of performance goal setting and evaluation reinforced the importance and objectivity of the system.

In addition, search engines and a variety of databases provided access to information about the company, its products, and the status of customer projects and internal company processes. Cross listings of people, projects, and skills provided tools that facilitated interaction and collaboration across the company.

### Putting the Customer First

Given the ambiguity of unit structure and strong accountability for performance, the key to making the organization's design work was a strong commitment to helping those who were helping customers.

There was little doubt that the key shared responsibility for everyone at Beta, Inc. was to help the customer. As one employee acknowledged, "If a customer has a need and it comes to our table, we own it—it becomes our first priority. You won't last very long at Beta if somebody asks you to help a customer and you ignore it." In a similar vein, another senior manager stated, "You can put up a red flag and say, 'I have a customer satisfaction problem.' Everyone drops everything to help you. Our goal of alignment around the customer makes it OK to cross boundaries."

These norms resulted in very wide spans of support for any customer-related issue or initiative. To help enforce this culture, senior managers spent a great deal of time reinforcing core values that emphasized shared responsibilities: focus on the customer, professional courtesy, integrity, and a bias for action. Moreover, widely dispersed share ownership (40 percent of equity was owned by employees) and heavy use of employee stock options made all employees feel like owners of the firm and allowed them to share in the benefits of success.

As discussed in chapter 6, to build a culture of shared responsibility to others, leaders must not only walk the talk but also hold subordinates accountable for demonstrated integrity and willingness to reach out and help others achieve important goals. The CEO at Beta constantly reinforced the importance of customer satisfaction by personally reviewing red-coded implementation issues and repeatedly saying that anyone could call at any time if it would help satisfy the needs of a customer. By acting as a role model and personally devoting a significant amount of his own time to tracking customer satisfaction and resolving customer issues, he reinforced the importance of the customer-based mission to everyone in the organization.

Reflecting on these norms and the culture they created, one employee noted, "Beta is a company where an excellent performer will be fired if he ignores the values of the company. Either you play by the rules or you're out."

### Adjusting the Levers to Support Beta's Strategy

Managers at Beta carefully adjusted the levers of organization design to support their strategy of delivering complex software

**FIGURE 7-5**

**Four Spans at Beta, Inc.**

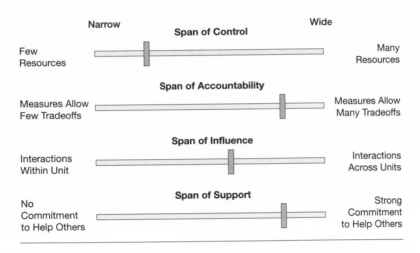

products and building customer loyalty. At a business strategy level, the four spans for Beta are illustrated in figure 7-5.

Beta's top managers chose a dedicated service relationship configuration to meet the needs of their large global customers. Given the complex nature of the product and its installation process, customer satisfaction was a function of resources—including third-party contractors—that Beta managers did not themselves control. Therefore, span of control was narrow and span of accountability was wide. The key customer satisfaction measure encompassed a wide range of tradeoffs affecting product design and delivery, installation and training, and after-sale service. Because span of accountability exceeded span of control, individuals were forced to become entrepreneurial in reaching out and working with many people throughout the business.

Information technology was used to support interactive networks created by stretch goals and an ambiguous organization structure. Transparency in goals and performance management allowed span of influence to widen as people were empowered to reach out to help others whose goals were aligned with their own. Finally, span of support was widened by strong norms that set out clear responsibilities: the customer comes first, and anyone who was not willing to help on a customer issue was deemed to be a poor fit for the company.

As with Alpha Co., senior managers at Beta adjusted the levers of organization design to help ensure the successful implementation of the company's unique strategy.

## EXAMPLE 3: GRADUATE SCHOOL OF BUSINESS ADMINISTRATION

The previous two examples have illustrated organizations with clear, profit-oriented business objectives. In this final example, we look at how the levers of organization design can be applied in a not-for-profit setting—in this case, a university business school.

What distinguishes this example is the relative importance of the "soft" side of organization design. Rather than focus primarily on unit structure and diagnostic control systems, managers of nonprofits rely much more extensively on wide spans of influence and support to implement strategies and achieve important goals.

### Metropolitan Business School

Metropolitan Business School (again, a disguised name) was a graduate school of business administration with fifteen hundred students enrolled in its two-year MBA program. The activities of the school encompassed research, doctoral programs, executive education, and a publishing division. The school employed 135 teaching faculty and 350 administrative staff.

Metropolitan Business School did not have an overall mission, although many of its programs and functions had specific mission statements that related to their specific activities. For example, the mission of the MBA program was to develop outstanding business leaders who would contribute to the well-being of society. The division of research and the doctoral programs had their own distinctive missions that focused on the creation of knowledge and communication with scholars in other universities.

### Customers in Knowledge Markets

Like all top-tier academic graduate schools, Metropolitan's primary customer was in knowledge markets—in this case, the professional academic community. Accordingly, Metropolitan's structure followed the expert knowledge configuration.

The unit structure at Metropolitan mirrored the specialized knowledge base of the underlying academic disciplines. The 135 faculty were grouped into eight academic units: Accounting and Control, International Business, Competition and Strategy, and so on. In this decentralized structure, each faculty group assumed responsibility for designing and delivering courses that reflected the paradigms and research interests of its discipline. Faculty units were also responsible for hiring, faculty development, and staffing courses.

As with all professional institutions, the allegiance of the professors was split between allegiance to Metropolitan Business School and allegiance to their academic disciplines. Identification with the disciplines was strong: faculty attended professional conferences to present their research, visited other universities to participate in seminars, published in peer-reviewed professional journals, and maintained a strong network of academic colleagues around the country. These professional peer networks were essential to academic success at Metropolitan: as a key element of the promotion process, professors at other universities were asked to evaluate the quality and impact of a Metropolitan professor's research.

In all professional institutions—hospitals, universities, and legal firms—there are two parallel structures: one set of unit groupings for professional workers, and another for staff support groups. Metropolitan Business School was no exception. Although the faculty were grouped by academic discipline, the 350 administrative staff members were grouped by product program and function. Thus, separate administrative units were created to support the MBA program, the doctoral program, the executive education program, publishing products, and alumni affairs. The administrative units were physically separated from the faculty buildings, and there was little interaction between the faculty and the administrative staff groups.

These administrative staff units assumed primary responsibility for meeting the needs of the constituents who contributed financial resources to the business school: students, executive education participants, and alumni. Consistent with most expert knowledge organizations, these constituents were not primary customers; nevertheless, they provided the revenue that allowed the institution to operate. Without their continuing support, faculty units would not be able to conduct the research that underpinned the school's ability to differentiate itself in knowledge markets. Accordingly, a great many administrative resources were devoted to ensuring that these constituents felt that their needs were adequately met.

### Limited Performance Measures

As with all nonprofit organizations, Metropolitan's senior managers had a difficult time designing control systems to create accountability for performance. Formal accountability systems worked well for administrative functions, but they were difficult to implement for faculty, who devoted their energy to research and course development.

Administrative staff units were managed like any support function in a traditional business setting. Units were managed as either revenue centers (alumni relations) or cost centers (the MBA program office). Administrators were responsible for delivering services within preset budget allocations. Some administrative units—for example, executive education and publishing—were managed as profit centers: managers of these activities were responsible for achieving revenue and net contribution targets.

The autonomous faculty units, in contrast, were neither given budgets nor held accountable for spending limits. Instead, resource expenditures were controlled primarily through headcount limits set by the dean, who had final authority for hiring and promotion decisions.

For professors, there was little correlation between measurable inputs (e.g., the number of hours spent on a research project or the number of classes taught) and the value of the outputs (e.g., the impact of new ideas and theories). And it was the latter—creativity and impact—that were the critical performance variables that determined Metropolitan's success. As a result, it was extremely difficult, if not impossible, to obtain valid measures of performance. An activity-based costing system compiled administrative and teaching hours for individual faculty members, but this data was not shared outside the dean's office.

Thus, as in other nonprofit settings, diagnostic control systems were relatively ineffective. How, then, was the implementation of strategy controlled and monitored? For this, we turn to the soft levers of interactive networks and shared responsibilities.

### Strong Interactive Networks

One of the unique features of many universities, including Metropolitan Business School, was the tenure system of faculty appointments, which granted lifetime employment for senior professors. Creative tension was needed to ensure that individuals sitting comfortably in their academic specialties worked together across units, focused sufficient attention on important constituents (e.g., students), and responded to the changing needs of business and society.

The principal way of coordinating effort and getting things done at Metropolitan was through interactive networks. Individual faculty members were constantly being asked by other faculty members or the dean to move outside their academic area units to serve on initiatives and task forces, join cross-disciplinary interest groups, teach in executive education programs, or assume responsibility for administering schoolwide programs.

At any time, a variety of task forces was at work studying schoolwide issues and formulating recommendations to the dean and the faculty. In addition, a number of important permanent cross-unit committees (e.g., the academic performance committee) met regularly, bringing together faculty from different parts of the school.

To move faculty out of their discipline-based silos, the dean had also created interest groups to bring together people from a variety of academic disciplines to study issues of mutual interest, such as the role of business in society or functional integration in complex business firms. Senior faculty members were also asked to serve as faculty heads of administrative units that dealt with constituents (e.g., executive education) or important support functions (e.g., the division of research). Thus, in addition to their teaching, research, and course development responsibilities (their "day" jobs), individual faculty members might be responsible for the administration of the MBA program or the publishing division.

Faculty members with large administrative assignments quickly found that their span of control was significantly less than their span of accountability: they were responsible for the success of complex programs or departments but had little control or decision rights over the faculty resources that they needed to accomplish their objectives. Consider, for example, a professor who was responsible for designing and delivering a new executive education program. He or she had to contact individuals in each academic area to ask whether they would be willing to participate. Unlike a business manager having a clear hierarchy and chain of command, the professor had no way to order compliance with such requests. Professors did not report directly to other faculty in the school. Accordingly, a commitment to help others was essential to make it all work.

The final mechanism for building interactive networks was the formal appointments process, which regularly brought together all senior faculty to review senior-level hiring and promotions. As a prelude to these meetings, which included all tenured professors, faculty from a variety of disciplines met in subgroups to evaluate candidates, debate faculty needs, and review the strategies of the individual faculty units. The appointments process met the four criteria for an interactive control system. The information generated through this process was an important and recurring agenda for the highest level of management (the university president and business school dean); the system demanded frequent and regular attention from all senior faculty; data was discussed in face-to-face meetings; and the process was used as a catalyst to continually challenge and debate the underlying assumptions of the school's direction and strategy. This highly interactive process demanded a great deal of faculty time, but it helped create influence networks that crossed traditional academic disciplinary boundaries.

### Commitment to Shared Purpose

One of the distinguishing features of a mission-focused organization is the willingness of individuals to help anyone who is committed to the organization's success.

Senior faculty frequently acted as role models, giving up their own time to help others succeed. The visible dedication of these senior professors—and the moral authority that they brought with their requests to help—made it difficult for more junior faculty members to turn down requests to participate in new teaching programs or interdisciplinary task forces for which they were responsible.

Teaching groups were designed to share best practices and help younger, less-experienced colleagues succeed in the classroom. Interest groups, committee assignments, teaching seminars, and mentoring were used to instill commitment to the broader institution and its mission. Over the years, these shared interactions created trust, friendships, and a sense of shared responsibilities.

A ten-year period of intensive indoctrination preceded promotion to full professor with tenure; this was sufficient time to test a candidate's commitment to the school's mission and his or her willingness to assume shared responsibility for its values and success.

To support this dense network of interaction, individual equity was managed very carefully. As discussed in chapter 6, resentment can quickly lead to an unwillingness to help others. To avoid this pitfall, the dean went to great lengths to ensure perceived equity among all faculty members. For this reason, individual workload metrics were not shared beyond the dean's office. No faculty members—even department heads—were granted access to data about activity levels of other faculty. Moreover, all faculty members were paid the same, based on a formula that recognized rank and years of service.

Pay for performance, a common practice in business, was studiously avoided. No school activity—whether teaching in executive education programs or assuming responsibility for performing an important administrative function—received extra compensation. Thus, when faculty members asked others to participate in an executive education program or head an administrative function, it would be asked in the context of performing service to support the mission of the school. Initiatives and tasks that did not support the mission of the school found little support from either the dean or the faculty.

## Adjusting the Levers to Support Metropolitan's Strategy

Metropolitan Business School was typical of many nonprofit organizations in the way that it used the levers of organization design. The four spans at Metropolitan are illustrated in figure 7-6.

Metropolitan's unit structure—an expert knowledge configuration—responded to the needs of its primary customers in the external academic community. But, like all nonprofit organizations, Metropolitan needed to satisfy important and powerful constituents: students, alumni, and corporate sponsors of executive education. In Metropolitan's case, these constituents supplied the revenue that allowed the organization to operate. To

**FIGURE 7-6**

## Four Spans at Metropolitan Business School

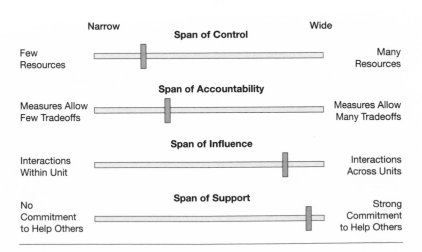

meet the needs of these groups, dedicated administrative staff units were created.

Span of control was generally narrow. Individual faculty members and unit heads did not have direct control of the resources they needed for success (some constituent-focused administrative units had wider spans of control). Metropolitan was typical in its lack of diagnostic control systems. It is inherently difficult to measure the value of outputs for knowledge-based professionals, whether professors in a business school, doctors in a hospital, or research scientists in an R&D laboratory. Limited accountability systems were in place for administrative units, and some student satisfaction data were collected but not widely shared. Instead of relying on diagnostic control systems to ensure the implementation of strategy, senior managers at Metropolitan emphasized strong interactive networks and wide spans of influence to move people beyond the silos of their academic disciplines and ensure coordination of complex tasks.

Wide spans of support were essential to allow these design choices to work. Because of a strong commitment to shared purpose, all faculty members felt a basic responsibility to help others. To support such norms, senior faculty acted as role models, and equity in work assignments and rewards was carefully managed.

Of course, this is not the only way that Metropolitan Business School could be managed. Instead of relying on interactive networks and shared responsibilities, senior managers might choose to manage the school more like a business—setting up business units, measuring outputs, and linking compensation to measures of performance. To implement this alternative approach, two obstacles would have to be overcome. First, diagnostic control systems would have to be developed that could generate valid and reliable measures of performance. As I have discussed, this is difficult for professional work, especially when research and creative course development are the critical variables of success. Second, senior managers would have to find ways to ensure that the recurring question is "What can I do to help?" rather than "What's in it for me?" They therefore would have to ensure that any inequity in compensation due to pay for performance or supplemental payments for designated tasks would not breed resentment that would quickly erode commitment to others and shared responsibilities.

## ADJUSTING THE LEVERS TOGETHER

The three examples in this chapter illustrate how the levers of organization design work together to enhance functioning and the achievement of strategy. In each of these three organizations, top managers made different choices—choices that seem appropriate for their circumstances. But in each case, the organization design was effective because all the levers were adjusted to reflect unique capabilities and strategies.

In the first two organizations—Alpha and Beta—managers emphasized unit groupings and diagnostic control systems, but they also aligned the softer levers to ensure that any potential resistance would not weaken the focus and energy created by these structures and systems. At Metropolitan Business School, as at most nonprofit organizations, formal systems were inherently less effective. Limitations in measurement and the autonomy of professional workers limited the extent to which diagnostic control systems could be relied on to ensure success. Instead, senior managers at Metropolitan put much more emphasis on the soft levers—interactive networks and shared responsibilities—to ensure that the goals of the organization were achieved.

Of course, these choices are neither inherently right nor inherently wrong. Nor are they static: they will change over time as circumstances change and as leaders change. But it should be clear from these three examples that managers must simultaneously adjust all four levers of organization design to implement strategy effectively.

It is now time to generalize the discussion. Chapter 8 offers a dynamic theory and a test that will allow you to ascertain whether the four levers are designed and adjusted correctly to ensure success in strategy implementation.

## CHAPTER THEME

The levers of organization design must be adjusted simultaneously to ensure the successful implementation of strategy.

## KEY CHAPTER IDEAS

- Depending on their unique circumstances, managers of successful organizations must devote different amounts of attention to the design of the hard and soft levers.

### Hard Levers
- Unit structure
- Diagnostic control systems

### Soft Levers
- Interactive networks
- Shared responsibilities

- The relative importance of the levers in different organizations—and the adjustment of their related spans—is a function of an organization's competitive environment and strategy.

## ACTION STEPS

1. Review the three examples here for similarities to your organization.

2. Consider how to adjust these levers to achieve alignment in your organization.

# 8

---

# Designing Organizations
## for Performance

Now that you have had a chance to review the mechanics of the different design levers, I am finally in a position to present an overarching framework and action principles for designing an organization for enduring performance.

Chapter 7 provided an overview of the design of three organizations to illustrate the levers and spans in action. The focus was to look at design principles at a high level—thirty thousand feet above ground. The goal in this chapter is to pull the analysis down to the level of individual people and business units to test whether different designs are capable of implementing strategy successfully.

Figure 8-1 summarizes the variables discussed so far in this book.

Starting with strategy in the upper-left corner, you can read down the four columns to review the steps that managers must follow to design an organization effectively:

**FIGURE 8-1**

## Shaping Span of Attention

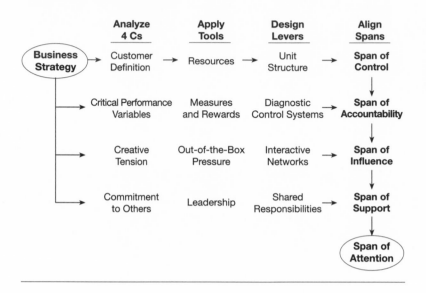

1. *Analyze the four Cs:*  Customer definition, critical performance variables, creative tension, and commitment to
   others. Based on the unique strategies that managers are
   attempting to implement, the following questions must
   be posed:
   - Who is the primary customer? What is the role of
     market-facing and operating-core units in creating
     value for this customer?
   - What are the relevant critical performance variables
     that define success? How should tradeoffs be reflected
     in performance measures?
   - How much creative tension is needed to stimulate in-
     novation and adaptation to changing circumstances?
   - How important is commitment to others in building
     customer loyalty and navigating organizational com-
     plexity?

2. *Apply the tools at hand:* Resources, measures and rewards, out-of-the-box pressure, and leadership.

3. *Design the four levers:* Unit structure, diagnostic control systems, interactive networks, and shared responsibilities.

4. *Align the four spans:* Span of control, span of accountability, span of influence, and span of support.

Although this step-by-step planning framework provides a useful summary, it falls short on two dimensions. First, these linear action steps fail to recognize the dynamic nature of the levers model. As figure 8-2 illustrates, these design variables are highly interdependent. Each variable is determined by and affects the others. Therefore, they cannot be designed or adjusted in isolation.

**FIGURE 8-2**

**Levers of Organization Design**

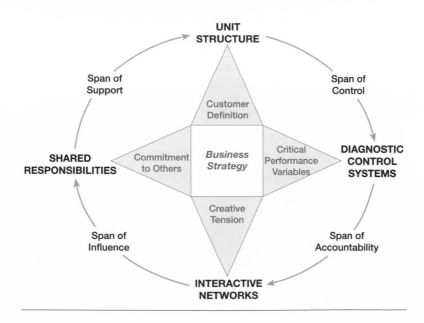

Second, you must remember that in designing organizations, the ultimate goal is to influence the *span of attention* of people on the ground—the many individuals whose work is essential to the successful implementation of strategy. Therefore, we must find a way to recognize both the interdependence of the model's variables and its primary focus on organizational attention.

## ARE THE SPANS ALIGNED?

Imagine various employees driving to work in the morning. As they think about the day ahead, their span of attention is determined by the things they need to accomplish. The following questions keep running through their minds:

1. What resources do I control to accomplish my tasks?

2. What measures will be used to evaluate my performance?

3. Who do I need to interact with and influence to achieve my goals?

4. How much support can I expect when I reach out to others for help?

To test whether an organization design will be successful in answering these questions in a way that ensures the implementation of key goals and strategies, we must change our vantage point. In the analysis in previous chapters, I have asked you to stand in the shoes of senior managers and pose the following question: "How can I design the different levers to support the implementation of our strategy?" To test whether span of attention for individuals throughout the organization is properly aligned and focused, you must now put yourself in the shoes of those people driving to work.

Taking an employee's perspective, you must split the diagram diagonally from lower left to upper right to separate the supply and demand of resources, as shown in figure 8-3.

**FIGURE 8-3**

**Demand and Supply of Organizational Resources**

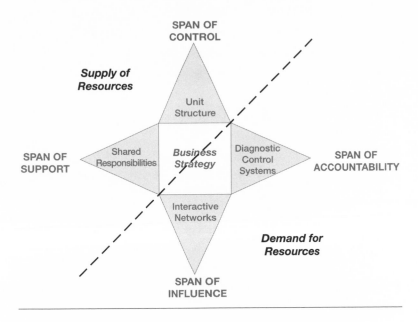

The upper-left half of figure 8-3—span of control and span of support—depicts the *supply of organizational resources* available to an individual. Span of control defines formal resources controlled directly by an individual: decision rights for people, physical facilities, information, and other tangible and intangible resources. But soft resources—in the form of span of support—are also critically important to the successful operation of any complex organization. As a result, in addition to understanding the resources that they control directly, individuals want to know the answer to the question, "To what extent can I count on people in other units to help me achieve my goals?"

The lower-right half of figure 8-3 represents an individual's *demand for organizational resources*. Span of accountability—defined by the tradeoffs embedded in diagnostic performance measures and incentives—creates demand for individuals to find the resources they need to achieve their goals: access to people, facilities, information, infrastructure, and so on. But demand for resources is also created by the out-of-the-box pressures of interactive networks: dual influence structures, stretch goals, and other mechanisms that cause people to widen their span of influence. Again, people are forced to ask, "Who do I need to interact with and influence to achieve my goals?"

Using the levers model, we can summarize the split between the supply of organizational resources and the demand for organizational resources as follows:

|  | | **"Hard" Levers** | **"Soft" Levers** |
|---|---|---|---|
| Supply of Resources | = | Span of Control | + Span of Support |
| Demand for Resources | = | Span of Accountability | + Span of Influence |

To achieve equilibrium in any setting where costly and scarce resources are in demand, the supply of resources must equal demand. Thus, an important test of successful organization design is the extent to which the sum of the demands that are placed on individuals through diagnostic control systems and interactive networks equals the sum of organizational resources available to those individuals through formal control of resources and informal support from others in the organization.

Put another way, the following equality must hold for a design to be sustainable:

$$\text{Span of Control} + \text{Span of Support} = \text{Span of Accountability} + \text{Span of Influence}$$

To illustrate this concept, consider the four spans at Mary Kay Inc. (top panel in figure 8-4). This consumer products company contracts with more than 1.3 million independent sales consultants to sell its well-known cosmetics and beauty products.

Consider first the supply of resources. The independent sales consultants control few direct resources and, as a result,

**FIGURE 8-4**

**Applying the X Test at Mary Kay**

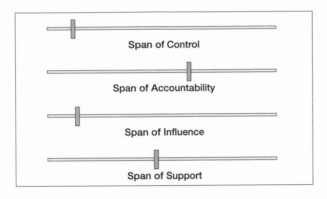

Span of Control

Span of Accountability

Span of Influence

Span of Support

**Spans in Equilibrium**

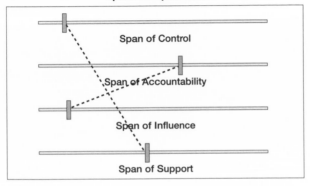

Span of Control

Span of Accountability

Span of Influence

Span of Support

have a narrow span of control. But span of support is relatively wide: the company supplies a broad range of training and sales tools to support each consultant. In addition, consultants attend weekly meetings that bring together other consultants and more experienced sales directors to share best practices and recognize and reinforce each other's success. Annual galas draw consultants from around the country to applaud each other's achievements. Recognition and financial rewards are carefully blended to reward and encourage success.

On the demand side of the equation, sales consultants are responsible for two measures that create a wide span of accountability: sales volume and the number of consultants recruited. Sales consultants are encouraged to act as entrepreneurs to achieve their volume and recruiting goals. Their span of influence, however, can be set quite narrow because their work is relatively self-contained: individual consultants use word of mouth and superior service to build their own networks of customers and recruits.

## The X Test

We can use figure 8-4 to test whether demand and supply of organizational resources are roughly in balance. To test equilibrium, we draw two lines: (1) one line that connects span of control and span of support (the supply of resources) and (2) a second line that connects span of accountability and span of influence (the demand for resources). When a design is in equilibrium—either at the individual, unit, or business level—these two lines will intersect. If they cross, as illustrated in the second panel of figure 8-4, then supply equals demand and the design is in alignment. If the lines do not cross, then the spans are misaligned and the organization design is out of balance—with predictable consequences. Either resources are insufficient to meet demand, suggesting a failure in strategy implementation, or resources exceed the needs of the organization, suggesting a lack of control and poor economic returns.[1]

Any organization chart can be redrawn to apply the alignment test to individual positions or units, or for the organization as a whole. A quick visual check of the spans in figure 8-5, for example, reveals that the spans for the various positions in this organization are aligned to create equilibrium: the lines joining the demand for resources (span of accountability and span of in-

**FIGURE 8-5**

## Organization Chart with Spans in Balance

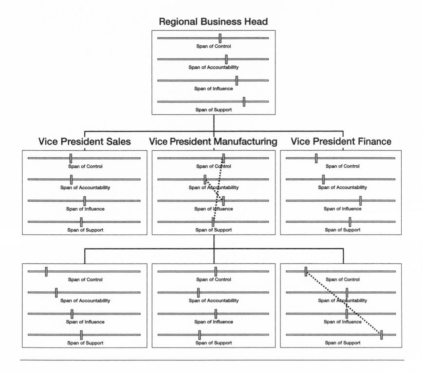

fluence) and the supply of resources (span of control and span of support) intersect to form an X. (For clarity, this test is illustrated for only two of the boxes on the organization chart.)

In practice, of course, we all know from personal experience that few organizations manage to get all this right all the time. Most organizations manage by muddling through with two or three of the basic design levers aligned. But as organizations become more complex, it becomes more important that all four levers of organization design are aligned. In principle, the more complex and demanding the task, the more resources that are required to execute it—and the spans shift farther to the right. But these resources cannot be deployed effectively unless the spans are adjusted according to analysis of the four Cs, and aligned to ensure that supply of organizational resources equals demand for those resources.

Recognizing that we are making broad generalizations to illustrate a point, we can test this equilibrium in a variety of settings. For example, we can compare the four spans in two highly regarded companies: Johnson & Johnson and General Electric (figure 8-6).[2] Johnson & Johnson is highly decentralized; it is organized into more than two hundred independent companies, each free to choose its own organizing structure based on unique markets and different primary customers. GE is more

**FIGURE 8-6**

**Comparing Spans for Market-Facing Managers at Johnson & Johnson and GE**

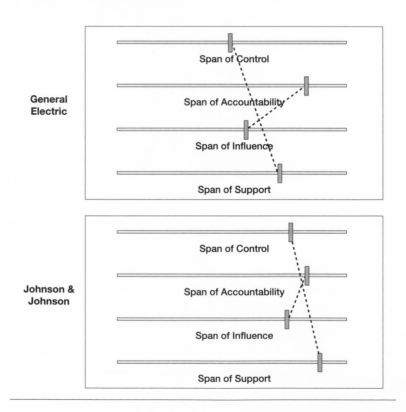

centralized; it is organized into a dozen sectors using a global standard of excellence configuration. Each company is designed uniquely, but both designs are well aligned.

Like all high-performing companies, both organizations have high expectations for performance: business managers are expected to make wide tradeoffs to achieve their goals. Accordingly, span of accountability for market-facing managers is wide in both organizations. Because of GE's centralized structure, however, span of control for its market-facing managers is narrower than at Johnson & Johnson. As a result, GE has a wider entrepreneurial gap: span of accountability is substantially greater than span of control. To achieve their goals, GE managers must become entrepreneurs within this large, complex organization.

To counteract the silos that are inevitable in GE's large, centralized organization, former CEO Jack Welch worked hard to ensure that span of influence was wider than span of control. Welch championed what he called a "boundaryless" organization and constantly extolled GE managers to think out of the box. To create interactive networks and widen span of influence, Welch installed a variety of dual influence structures (e.g., segment overlays) and cross-unit initiatives (e.g., workouts and six sigma quality programs). Span of support was also widened by a strong focus on mission and by the force of Welch's personality: he was vocal on the importance of shared responsibilities, and he personally reviewed the commitment of senior managers as a precondition for advancement.

Compared with GE market-facing managers, those at decentralized Johnson & Johnson have wider spans of control. As a result, the entrepreneurial gap at J&J is smaller: spans of control and accountability are relatively tightly aligned. To avoid complacency, J&J's top managers use their profit planning system interactively to infuse creative tension throughout the business. Driven by attention from the CEO and executive committee members ("everyone watches what the boss watches"), operating managers throughout Johnson & Johnson's business are required several times a year to follow an intensive bottom-up process to reestimate profit plans and five- and ten-year forecasts. Armed with new data, operating managers at all levels are continually challenged to develop action plans to respond to emerging threats or unanticipated opportunities.[3]

To ensure adequate spans of support for this interactive process, Johnson & Johnson promotes only from within, and managers are routinely transferred between businesses. Johnson & Johnson's credo, based on a foundation of responsibility to others, supplies the glue that holds the organization together: individuals know that they can reach out to others for help, with the full expectation that support will be there when needed.

Thus, you can see two different, but equally effective, approaches to aligning the four spans to balance the supply and demand of organizational resources. In each case, a visual check shows that the demand and supply lines intersect, indicating that the spans are in alignment.

## ADJUSTING THE SPANS DURING LIFE CYCLE CHANGES

In previous chapters, we used the work of an architect as a metaphor for organization design: surveying existing conditions, designing unit structures, specifying the electrical and power systems, and ensuring that the building supported the desired flow of human interaction.

It is now time to leave behind the metaphor of the architect. When an architect is satisfied with the outcome, the task is complete. He or she moves on to the next assignment. With organization design, however, there can be no fixed and final solution. Managers must ensure that their organization remains flexible and capable of change over time. To this end, Bower describes the benefits of creating a "Velcro" organization—one that is cohesive when in place but capable of easily being rearranged when circumstances and strategy change.[4]

To illustrate how the spans change during a typical firm's life cycle, we can revisit the stages of organizational growth model discussed in the opening pages of chapter 1 (compare figure 1-1 on page 4 with figure 8-7). In the early entrepreneurial growth

**FIGURE 8-7**

## Spans Change over Organizational Life Cycle

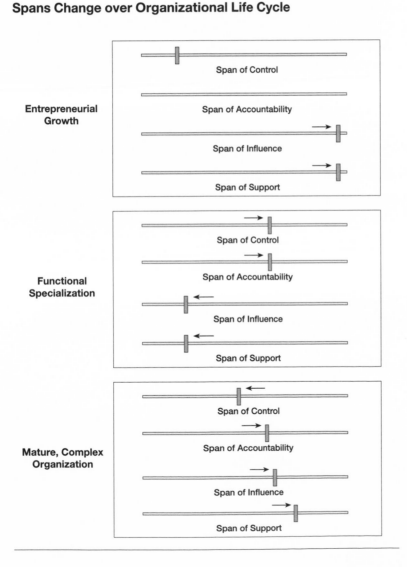

stage, span of control is very narrow because resources are scarce and no one controls all the resources needed to accomplish their job. At this formative stage, accountability systems are virtually nonexistent, so span of accountability is not an important variable in the analysis (and is omitted from figure 8-7). But narrow span of control and lack of formal accountability systems are compensated by very wide spans of influence and support: driven by excitement about the new venture and commitment to others on the team, everyone pitches in to help without the internal boundaries created by job titles or functional units.

During the next stage—when professional managers create functional units and install diagnostic control systems to instill discipline—span of control slides to the right: for the first time, resources are formally allocated to separate market-facing and operating-core units. Individuals heading up functional departments are given control of clearly defined resources. Span of accountability—created by newly installed diagnostic control systems—also becomes important at this stage and is tightly aligned to span of control. Because planning, coordination, and monitoring within functional units are now handled by formal structures and diagnostic control systems, span of influence and span of support become less important, and their sliders move to the left as these spans narrow.

In the mature stage, the organization has become large and complex. Now, strategy must be clearly defined so that managers can understand how to adjust the levers properly. The spans must be set separately for each position and unit with reference to the four Cs: customer definition, critical performance variables, creative tension, and commitment to others.

For self-contained positions, tight alignment of span of control and span of accountability is generally sufficient to achieve equilibrium between demand and supply. Such a situation may be encountered, for example, for manufacturing units that are insulated from the marketplace, or for Wall Street traders who settle their profit and loss accounts daily. In such cases, span of influence and span of support can be quite narrow. However, for many jobs—especially those that attempt to create customer loyalty within a complex organization structure—managers will intentionally create an entrepreneurial gap by setting span of accountability wider than span of control, forcing people to become entrepreneurs in their response to problems and opportunities. In this situation—illustrated in the bottom panel of figure 8-7—span of influence is also set wider than span of control to force people out of their silos. To allow this demanding design to work, span of support becomes critical, and its slider shifts to the right.

If the spans are significantly misaligned, strategy implementation will falter as people become confused, stifled, or isolated. We can anticipate the crises identified in the first pages of chapter 1 (as illustrated in the three panels of figure 8-8). The first crisis—a crisis of leadership—occurs in the rapidly growing entrepreneurial firm when spans of control and accountability are undefined and therefore do not supply the resources and direction needed to implement the strategy. This crisis is not reflected in figure 8-8 because typically it is caused by *lack* of organization design rather than misalignment of the spans.

In the functional organization in which managers attempt to instill discipline through structure and systems, a crisis of autonomy occurs if spans of accountability, influence, and support become so narrow that individuals cannot exercise their creative potential. In a highly decentralized organization, a crisis of control occurs when the supply of resources (span of control + span of support) exceeds management's ability to effectively monitor their use (span of accountability) and ensure coordination of activities and knowledge sharing with other units (span of influence). And, finally, in the large bureaucracy held together by

**FIGURE 8-8**

## Spans During Organizational Crises

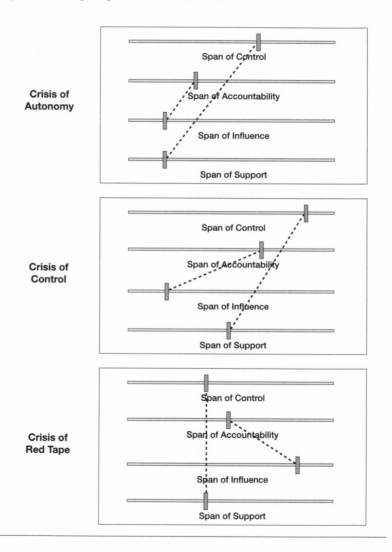

powerful staff groups supporting a segment structure, a crisis of red tape will occur when diagnostic and interactive systems (span of accountability + span of influence) become too complex for the organization that they are designed to support.[5]

Although underperformance is inevitable when the spans are out of balance, many managers still find it difficult to take up

the challenge of organization redesign. Organizational momen-
tum is a powerful force, and changing any of the design levers
risks disrupting the equilibrium that worked in the past. And
many large organizations, with their substantial stock of resources, can often survive for long periods even when the spans
are misaligned.

As a result, changes in the levers of design are often brought
about by revolution—the replacement of top management.
When existing management is unable or unwilling to adjust the
levers of design, new leaders are required.[6]

## REALIGNING THE SPANS AT IBM

To illustrate how managers redesign their organizations as
strategies and circumstances change, we can consider the history
of IBM and the design alignments that have been undertaken
there over the years (figures 8-9 and 8-10).[7]

IBM was founded in 1911, but its transformation to a large-
scale company of more than seventy thousand people occurred
under the leadership of Thomas J. Watson Sr., who was CEO
from 1924 until his death in 1956. Notwithstanding its large
size, IBM's structure was highly centralized. More than thirty
key functional and product executives reported directly to Watson, who approved every important decision. To build interactive networks that could bridge the functional structure, Watson
instituted a formal rotational program that required employees
to spend time in a variety of line and staff positions.

Tom Watson Sr. is remembered within IBM for creating a
formidable sales-based organization with a missionary focus on
the customer and for the responsibility to others that he embedded firmly in the organization through his emphasis on three
core values: respect for the individual, best possible customer
services, and superior performance. The top panel of figure 8-9
illustrates the spans for a typical market-facing unit during the

FIGURE 8-9

## Spans for IBM Market-Facing Unit Under Initial CEOs

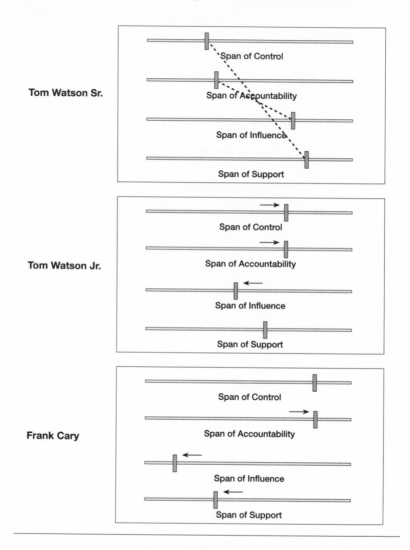

Tom Watson Sr.

Tom Watson Jr.

Frank Cary

leadership of Tom Watson Sr. (Note that the lines connecting supply and demand of resources intersect.)

Although IBM was extremely successful as a sales organization, by the end of Watson's tenure, many felt that IBM was falling behind in terms of technology and innovation. Tom Watson Jr. took over the company's leadership in 1956 and remained CEO until 1971. The younger Watson wanted to move away from the historical focus on tabulating machines and to reposition the company as a leader in computers. To improve market focus and innovation, Watson radically decentralized the business. He created new unit structures for a dozen global product families, each with a wide span of control and accountability. For the first time, product groups were run as profit centers. Because product families were largely self-contained, span of influence narrowed and shifted to the left.

To balance this shift and to ensure adequate spans of support for corporate and product initiatives, Watson changed executive compensation so that management bonuses were a function of overall IBM corporate performance. During this period, IBM introduced many new products and experienced its largest growth ever, swelling to more than a quarter million employees, based largely on the huge success of its System/360 mainframe computers. The effects of Tom Watson Jr.'s approach on a typical market-facing unit are illustrated in the second panel of figure 8-9.

By the early 1970s, the organization was feeling the effect of growth. When Frank T. Cary assumed leadership of IBM in 1972, he worried that IBM had become too big and too complacent. Cary believed that restructuring could be a catalyst for fresh thinking, and he pursued change as an end in itself. Cary became known for restructuring the business every two years: during this time, employees joked that IBM stood for "I've been moved." Convinced that distributed computing was the wave of the future, Cary created several new product divisions. Wide spans of accountability were pushed lower in the organization by the creation of a vast number of new profit centers. However, span of control was carefully aligned with span of accountability, and, as a result, there was little interunit dialogue or coordination. The organization was complex but housed in stand-alone

FIGURE 8-10

## Spans for IBM Market-Facing Unit, 1980–2005

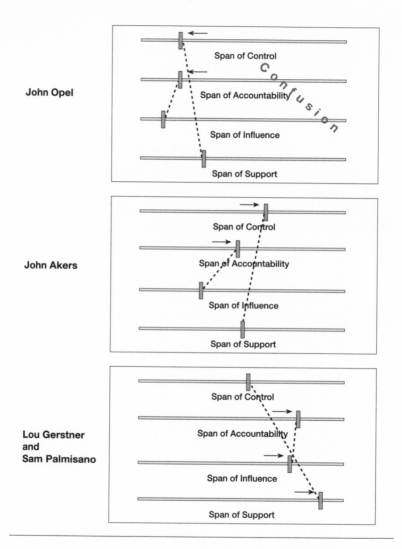

silos. Compensation was linked tightly to business unit financial results. Business unit managers were encouraged to compete with each other for resources, and that narrowed both span of influence and span of support (see the third panel of figure 8-9).

IBM's next CEO, for five years from 1980 to 1985, was John Opel. Reacting to threats from an ascendant Japanese computing industry, Opel again changed IBM's strategy, this time attempting to reposition the business as a low-price competitor. To drive cost efficiency, the business was reorganized on a functional basis. Span of control for operating-core units—notably manufacturing—was widened dramatically, with a corresponding reduction in span of control and span of accountability for market-facing sales units (top panel, figure 8-10). The definition of primary customer was also enlarged. Rather than focus narrowly on professional IT managers in large companies and governments, the company expanded the customer definition to include small companies, resellers, and distributors. Experimental "independent business units" were also created and were given resources to experiment without any accountability for performance.

By the end of Opel's tenure, IBM was criticized for confusion about who the primary customer was. As one writer noted, "IBM settled into a feeling that it could be all things to all customers."[8] Confusion reigned about strategy and priorities. More insidiously for long-term competitive health, the effects of these problems were masked by the dramatic and unrelenting growth of the computer industry. Given the apparent success of the corporation, IBM employees became arrogant, complacent, and insensitive to changing market conditions.

In 1985, John Akers took over an organization in trouble: IBM was bloated and out of touch with customers, and it was making inferior products. IBM's product lines emphasized hardware categories that were developed, manufactured, and marketed by independent functional silos. Not only were products incompatible across categories, but they also failed to meet customer needs in a world that was moving quickly away from hardware to software and customer solutions. To move closer to customers, Akers restructured by creating a new unified marketing and services group organized by geographic region. The mission of this market-facing unit was to translate customer needs into integrated product solutions and to coordinate internal resources to deliver the right products to customers. Business units and divisions were consolidated into six sectors, or lines of business. Span of control shifted dramatically to the right.

Span of accountability was also widened. Return on assets employed—a measure that allowed managers wide latitude and tradeoffs—became the primary financial performance indicator for senior executives. The new marketing and services group was given accountability for profit, and, as a result, many new profit centers were created. But span of accountability for market-facing units was not pushed far enough to the right. Managers were held accountable for new metrics including sales growth, line-item operating expenses, quality, and customer satisfaction. But the accounting system was not capable of calculating profit at the branch level or for individual customers and product lines. Instead, a top-down planning system set rigid sales quotas for each specific product category.[9]

By the early 1990s, with more than four hundred thousand employees, the organization had become complex and fragmented. Span of influence and span of support remained too narrow to provide the support needed for the changes that Akers was trying to implement. As losses continued to mount, Akers considered breaking the business into thirteen separate entities. Countless hours of management time were spent exploring this option.

Lou Gerstner took charge in 1993 and again changed the strategic direction of IBM. Instead of splitting up the business, he believed that "going to market as one IBM" would allow the company to capitalize on its unique strengths by offering integrated, customer-based solutions. He believed that IBM, with its many profit centers, had become too territorial and competitive. Accordingly, he restructured the business around specific industry groups, narrowing span of control and widening span of accountability for specific marketing units. To center the organization again on the primary customer—newly defined as senior-level decision makers in business and government responsible for creating value using IBM's products—Gerstner required each of IBM's top fifty executives to visit at least five customers within three months. To increase interactive networks, a dual influence structure was implemented: IBM global industry teams, who worked closely with customers, were formally paired with product specialists. To widen span of support, bonuses were reconfigured to give more weight for IBM corporate results than for individual unit results. By the end of his tenure in 2002, IBM's strategy was clearly defined as the provision of integrated services.

Sam Palmisano took over as CEO in 2002. The new strategic position articulated by Palmisano emphasized responsive "on-demand" computing solutions delivered through seamless integration of hardware, software, and services. Palmisano reorganized by adopting a dedicated service relationship configuration and began using the term *clients* instead of *customers* to signal the long-time relationships that the new strategy was designed to foster.[10] To ensure that all employees in this highly complex organization would be willing to work across their defined units to build customer loyalty, Palmisano further widened spans of support. Palmisano returned the company to its roots by reemphasizing the importance of IBM values regarding shared responsibilities.[11] To increase perceived equity—an important precondition if people are to assume responsibility to help others—Palmisano asked the board to allocate half of his 2003 bonus to other IBM executives who would be critical leaders of the new team-based strategy.

## Two Types of Design Interventions

As IBM's history illustrates, organization designs can be changed in a variety of ways. Design interventions can fall on a continuum from evolutionary—adjustments focusing primarily on the soft levers of interactive networks and shared responsibilities—

to revolutionary, with changes focusing primarily on the hard levers of unit structure and diagnostic control systems.

## Soft Intervention

If an organization is well positioned in its competitive market, senior managers may not wish to change their basic design structure. But they may still want to change the patterns of action within the organization. For example, they may want more consumer focus, more innovation, faster speed to market, or more cross-unit collaboration. In the absence of a major restructuring, the main levers of intervention in such circumstances are the soft levers: interactive networks and shared responsibilities.

Typically, the first step in a soft intervention is to increase creative tension and interactive networks through dual influence structures: task forces, cross-unit groups, and dotted line relationships. Managers can also introduce creative tension through formal systems—stretch goals, cross-unit cost allocations, and interactive control systems—to foster interactive networks.

If commitment to others is essential for success, leaders will also attempt to build a sense of shared responsibilities. Through their words and deeds, senior managers will work to communicate responsibility to customers (or other critical constituents) and emphasize the importance of helping others who are supporting the customer-focused mission. Managers will publicly recognize and promote role models. Human resource policies will favor promotion from within along with formal job rotation programs. Managers will typically change incentives to reward group and corporate-level performance.

By increasing creative tension and commitment to others, soft interventions can be very effective in changing patterns of action. But such interventions will fail if there is lack of clarity about the other two Cs: customer definition and critical performance variables. If customer focus and accountability measures are unclear, then confusion surrounding the hard levers—unit structures and diagnostic control systems—will inevitably derail change efforts.

## Hard Intervention

At the opposite end of the spectrum, senior managers may decide that the organization needs to be repositioned to respond to changing competitive dynamics. A major redesign will be necessary, for example, if managers want to shift the organization's focus to a new primary customer, a new basis of differentiation, or wholly new product categories that need support.

In a hard intervention, managers redraw the organization chart to redefine market-facing and operating-core units and to reallocate resources. Often, they will adopt a new structural configuration. This surgical approach leads to the most dramatic upheaval as spans of control are realigned and new accountabilities are assigned to individual managers and units. Some managers find that they now control more resources, whereas others find that their span of control has narrowed. As a result, this type of interaction creates high levels of anxiety (and, sometimes, creative tension).

Managers may intentionally modify unit structures and accountability targets to force people to rethink their plans. John Browne, CEO of oil giant BP, described the process:

> To create an effective learning organization, you don't bolt things down. You let the organization and the ways in which it learns evolve. If you don't, organizational structures can become obstacles to the free flow of knowledge and can become disconnected from the business purpose. When I headed BPX, I set new targets every two years or so and then

changed the structure and some of the people in order to deliver the targets. Why? Because I think you have to impose discontinuous change until you can see that the organization will discontinuously change itself.[12]

But as we have discussed at length, performance measurement systems must be capable of supporting these new designs. Measures, goals, and incentive systems must be supported by diagnostic and interactive control systems that are aligned with the new structure and can provide information for control and learning. Access to reliable, transparent data is essential. As our alignment X test reminds us, however, hard interventions are unlikely to succeed over the long term unless the soft levers— interactive networks and shared responsibilities—are also designed carefully to ensure that the supply and demand of resources in the new organization are in balance.

## THE ALLURE OF THE MATRIX

In any complex organization operating in competitive markets, a matrix organization is an appealing design solution because it allows simultaneous focus on multiple dimensions of value creation. Rather than choose to focus primarily on product excellence, regional customization, or scale efficiencies, managers can adopt a matrix structure to give equal weight and attention to two or more of these dimensions.

Many companies have attempted a matrix structure, but most of them have failed. The equilibrium analysis in this chapter unlocks the reason. As shown in the discussion of Alpha Co. in chapter 7, a successful matrix organization must have all four spans set very wide. The more demanding the organization and its strategy, the more organizational resources it will require for successful implementation of strategy—and the more managers

FIGURE 8-11

## Spans for a Matrix Design

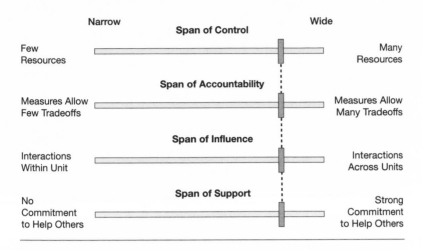

must shift the sliders to the right (figure 8-11). Senior managers must give control of a wide range of resources to decentralized operating-core and market-facing units; performance measures must be designed both to ensure strict accountability for results and to allow high-level business tradeoffs; managers must supplement dual influence structures with supporting cost allocation, transfer-pricing, and interactive control systems; and a sense of shared responsibility and a bias for action must permeate the organization.

All this is, of course, possible. But the potential for problems is very high in any organization where all four spans are both very wide and so tightly aligned that they are stacked vertically. Although the design may be temporarily in balance, the equilibrium is precarious. When spans are in equilibrium with more "spread," managers can often make a change in any one span without disturbing the balance. But for a matrix, a relatively small change in any single lever will disrupt the balance of supply and demand and will tip the organization toward disequilibrium.

In a matrix, the ideal positioning of the spans is commonly thwarted for one or more of the following reasons:

- *Span of control:* Lack of clarity about who controls resources or who has decision rights for their deployment

- *Span of accountability:* Inability of accounting and IT systems to aggregate business-level performance data for operating-core and market-facing units along each dimension of the matrix (e.g., product and region)

- *Span of influence:* Unequal access to performance information, leading to power imbalances in dual influence structures; inability to accurately allocate indirect costs to all units and establish adequate transfer-pricing policies between them

- *Span of support:* Lack of commitment to others, as evidenced by lack of shared responsibilities focusing on customers, teamwork, and rapid decision making

To make a matrix work, senior managers have little room for error: not only must resources be clearly allocated with commensurate accountability, but also managers at all levels must be highly skilled and the organization must have sophisticated information technology and performance management capabilities.

## Recognizing Human Needs

This book has focused primarily on the formal side of organizations: the formal grouping of resources dedicated to achieving specific aims. But it would be folly—and presumptuous—to think that the structures and systems that we design are sufficient to guarantee success.

We must remember that formal systems and structures are a starting point and not an ending point. They merely set the stage and provide the backdrop for individual human initiative. In fact, the most important ingredient in any organization design is the ability to preserve the spontaneous human ingenuity that can figure out how to create new opportunities and overcome obstacles along the way.

We must also remember that organizations are singularly human inventions—designed by humans to coordinate and focus the energies of humans. Different designs require people with different skills, aptitudes, and preferences. But regardless of these differences, if any organization is to succeed and endure, it must respond to the basic human needs of the people who populate it.

To conclude the analysis, therefore, we must consider one final test: the extent to which a potential design meets the human needs of the people who work within it. Although there are many ways to describe the psychological and physical bases of human nature, Lawrence and Nohria argue, in a compelling analysis, that the biological needs of humans can be represented by four basic drives:[13]

- The drive to acquire

- The drive to defend

- The drive to learn

- The drive to bond

Let's explore how our model responds to these needs. The first drive—the drive to acquire—is the essence of competitive markets. We must never forget the power of self-interested individuals working for personal gain. The drive to acquire is reflected in our model in unit structures and span of control. Control of resources brings wealth, status, and a sense of personal accomplishment. The control of these resources also signals status to important reference groups: coworkers, family, and friends. To be attractive places for managers and employees to work, organizations must offer individuals the opportunity to control organizational resources and to receive salaries or bonuses that enhance their personal wealth.

The drive to defend represents the basic need for safety and for the protection of things of value: personal property, relationships, reputation, and self-esteem. Any substantial threat provokes a defensive reaction in humans. For organizations to survive and adapt over time, early warning systems must exist to alert individuals of threats to personal and organizational goals. In our model, these needs are met by diagnostic control systems and span of accountability. These systems must provide early warning systems for surprises and give individuals the freedom to make tradeoffs to ensure that assets and individual achievements are secure.

The drive to learn represents the basic human need to make sense of the world. Human advancement is based on knowledge and learning, much of it transmitted through abstract symbols. Curiosity combined with human ingenuity is a powerful, and virtually limitless, human force. Interactive networks and span of influence respond to the drive to learn. Organizations—with their resources, products and services, and potential—must provide individuals with an outlet to exercise their innate desire to create, experiment, improve, and learn.

Finally, the drive to bond reflects the social nature of human beings. Continuing interaction with others and mutual commitments of support are basic human needs. In our model, the drive to bond is reflected in shared responsibilities and span of support. Individuals rely on organizations to create bonds of mutual support through affiliation and friendships. To be successful and sustainable, organizations must offer participants the opportunity to interact with others who can provide a sense of sharing and belonging—not only to one or more of the individual subgroups that make up the organization but also to the purpose, history, and culture embodied by the organization itself.

The power of the four biological drives derives not only from the specific behaviors created by each drive but also, more fundamentally, from their interaction. For example, the tension between the drive to acquire and the drive to bond shapes the degree to which people act selfishly or selflessly in different circumstances: our behavior when negotiating the purchase of a new car is very different from the way we behave when negotiating with our family or friends about a vacation venue. Similarly, the tension between the drive to learn and the drive to defend shapes the way we respond to information that challenges our self-image.

Just as the power of human drives lies in their interaction, the power of the levers of organization design derives from the tension that exists among them. Wanting more (span of control) is sometimes in conflict with the responsibility to help others (span of support). The desire to defend (diagnostic control systems) can be at odds with the desire to engage others to learn (interactive networks). The power of organizations—and their unequaled ability to create value—is fueled in large part by these dynamic tensions.

## THE RESPONSIBILITY OF LEADERS

The art of progress is to preserve order amid change,
and to preserve change amid order.[14]

One of the strongest messages in management theory over the past thirty years is the dictum that an organization's structure—its design—should be a function of its specific strategy. It is true, I believe, that organization design is management's primary tool for focusing and aligning resources to ensure the implementation of business objectives and strategies.

However, structure is not merely a passive reflection of strategy. More fundamentally, organization design affects people—how they relate to each other and how they question assumptions, experiment, and learn. If a design doesn't recognize this tension—between allocating resources to implement today's strategies and creating pressures for people to adapt for tomorrow—then the scarcest resources of any organization—its people, knowledge, and information processing capabilities—cannot be leveraged effectively.

I have defined organization design as the formal system of accountability that defines key positions in an organization and legitimates rights to set goals, receive information, and influence the work of others. Much of the discussion in this book has focused on how to infuse this formal system of accountability throughout the organization so that individuals several levels removed from top management can understand their roles in the organization and their rights to set goals, receive information, and influence the work of others.

I end this book by reminding you that leaders must assume personal responsibility for organization design: defining the customer, identifying and monitoring critical performance variables, injecting creative tension in the business, and setting a level of commitment to others that supports the organization's strategy and shared values.

Managers can reach out to consultants and staff experts for help in designing the hard levers—defining the customer and identifying critical performance variables. For these variables, sophisticated analytic techniques can be very useful. But the soft levers—which I have argued are just as important, and sometimes more important—require the will of leadership if they are to be implemented effectively. Consultants and staff specialists can do little more than assist. Leaders must lead the way.

Organizations are critically important to individuals and to society. They not only supply the goods and services that underpin our economy and governments, but they also give meaning to our work and to our lives. As a result, those who lead organizations—large and small—must recognize and assume this vital responsibility.

Using the levers of organization design to dynamically align the four spans is the essence of designing organizations for performance.

- The ultimate goal of organization design is to influence the span of attention of each individual in an organization.

- To balance the four spans, equilibrium must be achieved between the demand for resources and the supply of resources—encompassing both the hard and the soft levers.

- Alignment can be tested by drawing separate lines between (1) span of control and span of support and (2) span of accountability and span of influence. When the spans are in alignment, the two lines will intersect, forming an X.

- Alignment of the four spans will change over time depending on the life cycle stage of the organization and the strategy that senior managers want to implement.

- Managers can intervene to align the spans using either a soft intervention (focusing on the soft levers: interactive networks and shared responsibilities) or a hard intervention (focusing on the hard levers: unit structure and diagnostic control systems).

- Successful organization designs must respond to four basic human drives:
  - The drive to acquire
  - The drive to defend
  - The drive to learn
  - The drive to bond

- Designing their organizations is the primary responsibility of all leaders.

## ACTION STEPS

1. Decide on the unit of analysis:
   - Position or job
   - Unit grouping (e.g., market-facing or operating-core unit)
   - Business

2. Analyze the four Cs:
   - Customer definition
   - Critical performance variables
   - Creative tension
   - Commitment to others

3. Based on analysis of the four Cs, apply the tools at hand:
   - Resources
   - Measures and rewards
   - Out-of-the-box pressure
   - Leadership

4. Design the levers:
   - Unit structure
   - Diagnostic control systems
   - Interactive networks
   - Shared responsibilities

5. Adjust the spans:
   - Span of control
   - Span of accountability
   - Span of influence
   - Span of support

6. Using the X test, ensure that the supply of organizational resources equals the demand for those resources:

$$\frac{\text{Span of}}{\text{Control}} + \frac{\text{Span of}}{\text{Support}} = \frac{\text{Span of}}{\text{Accountability}} + \frac{\text{Span of}}{\text{Influence}}$$

7. Readjust the spans to maintain a dynamic equilibrium with changing strategies and circumstances.

# NOTES

*Preface*

1. From a review by Goold and Campbell, *Designing Effective Organizations*, 337.

*Chapter 1*

1. Prokesch, "Unleashing the Power of Learning," 19.
2. Coleman, *Foundations of Social Theory*, 4.
3. Greiner, "Evolution and Revolution as Organizations Grow."
4. In Greiner's article, the final stage is not the back-to-basics phase described here but rather the "collaborative organization." Greiner was hopeful that the last, collaborative stage would be a successful solution to the design challenges that were inadequately addressed in earlier stages.
5. Miller and Friesen, *Organizations: A Quantum View*, 90–101.
6. Brickley et al., *Designing Organizations to Create Value*, 55–59.
7. Ibid., 16–17.
8. Erik Gunnar Counselman, "The US Marine Corps: Responsibility to Others and Commitment to Mission" (MBA paper, Harvard Business School, December 2004).

*Chapter 2*

1. The five Ps of strategy—position, plans, patterns, perspective, and ploy—are from Mintzberg, "Five Ps for Strategy." We focus

on the first four Ps and leave strategy as ploy to those who specialize in game theory.

2. Porter, *Competitive Strategy*; Porter, *Competitive Advantage*.

3. Presentation by Jerald G. Fishman, CEO, Analog Devices, at the Strategic Management Society Conference, San Juan, November 1, 2004.

4. Simons, *Performance Measurement & Control Systems for Implementing Strategy*, 53.

5. Weber, *The Protestant Ethic and the Spirit of Capitalism*, 329–341.

6. Chandler, *Strategy and Structure*.

7. Simon, *Administrative Behavior*.

8. Galbraith, *Organization Design*.

9. Lawrence and Lorsch, *Organization and Environment*.

10. Mintzberg, *The Structuring of Organizations*; Miller and Friesen, *Organizations: A Quantum View*.

### Chapter 3

1. Kramer, *Organizing for Global Competitiveness*, 7–8.

2. Sheth et al., *Customer Behavior*, 5, 12.

3. Shuman et al., *Everyone Is a Customer*, 1.

4. Massnick, *The Customer Is CEO*, 7.

5. GE Annual Report 1990, as reported in Sheth et al., *Customer Behavior*, 16.

6. In government organizations, where positions are filled by elected officials and their appointees, the political process influences strongly how resources are allocated. Accordingly, in such circumstances it is essential to have structural checks and balances in place to ensure that the interests of constituents are protected. For a discussion of these issues, see Wilson, *Bureaucracy*, chapters 7 and 11.

7. When these conditions are met, the next logical question is why the internal function is not spun off as a separate stand-alone entity. In other words, what is the economic rationale for keeping these units in the firm?

8. Mintzerg, *The Structuring of Organizations*, 19.

9. There is a large literature regarding span of control, most of it debating how many people should optimally report to a manager. Management books typically argue that span of control should be broad—that is, many subordinates reporting to one manager—when work is routine, workers are skilled, and rules and procedures are adequate to achieve coordination (Galbraith et al., *Designing Dynamic*

*Organizations*, 91). For a summary of this literature, see Perrow, *Complex Organizations*, 30–33, and Mintzberg, *The Structuring of Organizations*, 134–135.

10. Simons, *Performance Measurement & Control Systems for Implementing Strategy*, 50.

11. Quotation from Decker, *Winning with the P&G 99*, 152. Cited in Kirsten Paust, "The Organizational Design Choices of IBM, Southwest Airlines, and P&G" (individual MBA research study, Harvard Business School, April 2003). It should be noted that Procter & Gamble reorganized in 2000 to a matrix organization structure (to be discussed in later chapters).

12. *New York Times*, October 12, 2003: BU11.

13. Full-page ad in *Fortune*, February 2003.

14. S. Lohr, "Big Blue's Big Bet: Less Tech, More Touch," *New York Times*, January 25, 2004: BU 10.

15. Ibid.

16. Mintzberg, *The Structuring of Organizations*, 124.

17. Vikram Punwani, "Learning Organization Design from Southwest: Teamwork in the Investment Management Industry" (MBA paper, Harvard Business School, December 2003).

18. Tor Minesuk, "Less Is More: The Organization Design of a Mutual Fund Company" (MBA paper, Harvard Business School, December 2004). It should be noted that this internal definition of primary customer can be dangerous if resources are inappropriately dedicated to serving the needs of star investment managers. For example, the biasing of supposedly independent research advice to enhance deal flows for star bankers led to scandals and fines levied against ten global investment banks in 2003. (Y Wu, "Equity Research—Post Spitzer Organizational Realignment" (MBA paper, Harvard Business School, December, 2004)).

19. Garett Poston, untitled MBA paper (Harvard Business School, September 2003).

20. D. Grainger, "Can McDonald's Cook Again?" *Fortune*, April 14, 2003: 124.

21. Bradach, *Franchise Organizations*, 21–22.

22. S. Day, "After Years at Top, McDonald's Strives to Regain Ground," *New York Times*, March 3, 2003: A19.

23. Jim Cantalupo, quoted in Grainger, "Can McDonald's Cook Again?": 120.

24. S. Day, "After Years at Top, McDonald's Strives to Regain Ground."

25. R. Tomkins, "As Hostility Towards America Grows, Will the World Lose Its Appetite for Coca-Cola, McDonald's and Nike?" *Financial Times*, March 27, 2003: 13.

26. R. Guth, "Midlife Correction: Inside Microsoft, Financial Managers with More Clout," *Wall Street Journal*, July 23, 2003: A1.

27. Kristin Lambert, untitled MBA paper (Harvard Business School, September 2003).

28. Katya Chashechkina, "Designing Intel for Growth and Innovation" (MBA paper, Harvard Business School, December 2003).

29. Mikio Fujitsuka, "Honda Motor Company" (MBA paper, Harvard Business School, December 2003).

30. J. Mackintosh, "Paying the Bill After the Price War," *Financial Times*, September 30, 2004: 8; L. Hawkins Jr., "Reversing 80 Years of History, GM Is Reining in Global Fiefs," *Wall Street Journal*, October 6, 2004: A1.

31. William E. Coyne, senior vice president, research and development, 3M (Minnesota Mining and Manufacturing Company), quoted in Kanter et al., *Innovation*, 55.

32. Felicia Lim, "How and Why Ingersoll-Rand Uses Organization Design to Achieve Its Strategy" (MBA paper, Harvard Business School, December 2003).

33. The term *satisfice*, coined by Nobel laureate H. A. Simon, refers to the human tendency to seek a result that is good enough, although not necessarily the best that could be achieved in the circumstances. In Simon's own words, "Administrative theory is peculiarly the theory of intended and bounded rationality—of the behavior of human beings who *satisfice* because they have not the wits to *maximize*." (*Administrative Behavior*, 3rd edition, New York, The Free Press, 1976: xxvii. Italics in original.)

34. Treacy and Wiersema, *The Discipline of Market Leaders*, 33.

35. J. I. Cash, "Otis Elevator: Managing the Service Force," Case 191–213 (Boston: Harvard Business School, 1991).

36. D. Kirkpatrick, "Inside Sam's $100 Billion Growth Machine," *Fortune*, June 14, 2004.

37. J. Useem, "One Nation Under Wal-Mart," *Fortune*, March 2, 2003: 74; C. L. Hayes, "What They Know About You: An Obsessive Monitor of Customer Behavior," *New York Times*, November 14, 2004: BU1.

38. Quoted in Magretta, "The Power of Vertical Integration," 78–79, 83.

39. S. Morrison, "Radical Who Believes Age Is Not a Virtue," *Financial Times*, Information Technology Review Section, March 3, 2004: 2.

40. Rebecca Wahl, "Amazon.com: Serving the Customer" (MBA paper, Harvard Business School, December 2003).

41. R. Guth, "Midlife Correction: Inside Microsoft, Financial Managers with More Clout," *Wall Street Journal*, July 23, 2003: A1.

### Chapter 4

1. Named after German physicist Georg Simon Ohm (1789–1854).

2. Craig Mundie, as reported in B. Schlender, "Ballmer Unbound," *Fortune*, January 26, 2004: 123.

3. For a complete discussion of the properties of good measures, see Simons, *Levers of Control*, 75–78.

4. For detailed information on the use of the financial accountability wheels, see Simons, *Performance Measurement & Control Systems for Implementing Strategy*, chapter 5.

5. Depending on the business, the cash wheel may encompass other variables such as market investments.

6. Quoted in Magretta, "The Power of Vertical Integration," 81.

7. To isolate after-tax operating income, net income for the ROCE calculation is often defined as EBIAT (earnings before interest charges but after taxes).

8. For details on replacement cost accounting and how to compute ROCE, residual income, and EVA, see Simons, *Performance Measurement & Control Systems for Implementing Strategy*, chapters 5 and 8.

9. Quoted in S. London, "Enterprise Drives Home the Service Ethic," *Financial Times*, June 2, 2003: 7.

10. Simons, *Levers of Control*, 59.

11. For a complete discussion, see Simons, *Levers of Control*, chapter 4, and Simons, *Performance Measurement & Control Systems for Implementing Strategy*, chapter 10.

12. Simons, *Levers of Control*, 63.

13. Kaplan and Norton, *The Balanced Scorecard*, 31.

14. For techniques related to this approach, see Kaplan and Norton, *The Balanced Scorecard*.

15. The arithmetic decomposition of ROE was devised by Donaldson Brown, chief financial officer of DuPont, in 1915. See Johnson and Kaplan, *Relevance Lost*, 86, 101.

16. Stevenson and Jarillo, "A Paradigm of Entrepreneurship," 23.

17. S. Greenhouse, "Wal-Mart, A Nation Unto Itself," *New York Times*, April 17, 2004.

18. Of course, senior managers may choose to widen both span of accountability and span of control to encourage more entrepreneurial behavior. At Wal-Mart, for example, in addition to the detailed performance metrics described here, managers are accountable for store profit (thereby widening span of accountability) and have the right to lower (but not raise) prices to respond to local competition (widening span of control).

19. Hackman, *Leading Teams*, 78.

20. Kanter et al., *Innovation*, 18.

21. Brickley et al., *Designing Organizations to Create Value*, 137.

22. Simons, *Levers of Control*, 117–119.

23. Simons and Dávila, "How High Is Your Return on Management?"

24. Kerr, "On the Folly of Rewarding A While Hoping for B."

25. Taylor, "Principles and Methods of Scientific Management," 117–124.

26. William E. Coyne, senior vice president, research and development, 3M (Minnesota Mining and Manufacturing Company), quoted in Kanter et al., *Innovation*, 53.

27. Campbell et al., "Using Non-Financial Measures for Evaluating Business Strategy."

28. J. Greene, "Ballmer's Microsoft: How CEO Steve Ballmer Is Remaking the Company That Bill Gates Built," *Business Week*, June 17, 2002.

29. Applegate et al., *Corporate Information Strategy and Management*.

30. Simons, *Performance Measurement & Control Systems for Implementing Strategy*, 269–273.

31. Simons, *Levers of Control*.

**Chapter 5**

1. Milgrom and Roberts, *Economics, Organization, and Management*, 192; Brickley et. al., *Designing Organizations to Create Value*, 92–94.

2. Levitt, "Creativity Is Not Enough," 143.

3. Van De Ven et al., "Determinants of Coordination Modes Within Organizations."

4. Quoted in P. Sellers, "eBay's Secret," *Fortune*, October, 18, 2004: 162.

5. Lewis S. Edelheit, quoted in Kanter et al., *Innovation*, 101–102.

6. Kurt Scherer, "An Analysis of a US Marine Corps Attack Helicopter Squadron" (MBA paper, Harvard Business School, December 2003).

7. M. Beer and P. L. Fagan, "Merck & Co., Inc.: Corporate Strategy, Organization, and Culture (A) and (B)," Cases 9–499-054 and 9–499-046 (Boston: Harvard Business School, 1999).

8. Kanter et al., *Innovation*, 154–155.

9. Bradach, *Franchise Organizations*, 47.

10. William E. Coyne, senior vice president, research and development, 3M (Minnesota Mining and Manufacturing Company), quoted in Kanter et al., *Innovation*, 55.

11. See Simons, *Performance Measurement & Control Systems for Implementing Strategy*, chapter 11, for a full discussion.

12. C. A. Bartlett and M. Wozny, "GE's Two-Decade Transformation: Jack Welch's Leadership," Case 9–399-150 (Boston: Harvard Business School, 1999). Reported by Cyrus D'souza, "GE in the Post Jack Welch Era" (MBA paper, Harvard Business School, December 2004).

13. Prokesch, "Unleashing the Power of Learning," 158.

14. J. Podolny and J. Roberts, "Performance Management and Learning at British Petroleum," unnumbered case (Stanford, CA: Stanford University Graduate School of Business, 2004).

15. Prokesch, "Unleashing the Power of Learning," 152.

16. Because of the risk of information biasing or manipulation, effective controls are essential when performance pressures are high. For a discussion of how to diagnose performance pressure risks, see Simons, "How Risky Is Your Company?" For a discussion of how to implement controls and safeguards, see Simons, *Levers of Control*.

17. Dent, "Tensions in the Design of Formal Control Systems," 135.

18. For a discussion of the controllability principle, see Merchant, *Control in Business Organizations*, 21.

19. Vancil, *Decentralization: Managerial Ambiguity by Design*, 105, 118.

20. For a summary, see Eccles, *The Transfer Pricing Problem*.

21. Using standard variable cost, rather than actual cost, properly assigns accountability for efficiency variances to the producing unit.

22. Janet Huang, untitled MBA paper (Harvard Business School, November 2004).

23. We should note, however, that allowing unit managers to divert goods and services to outside markets fails to reflect the synergies and economies that accrue from shared resources and favorable contracting inside the firm. This approach ignores the strategic reasons that senior corporate managers chose to house the various units of the firm under one roof in the first place. For example, a strategy of vertical integration may reflect the economic and strategic benefits that accrue from mating the sources of supply with manufacturing and distribution channels. The creation of a pure market-oriented transfer-pricing system in such an organization raises the question of whether the organization would not be better served by spinning off these units and dealing with them as external entities.

24. Simons, *Levers of Control*, 95.

25. Ibid., 108–109.

26. Simons, "Strategic Orientation and Top Management Attention to Control Systems."

27. J. Scully, *Odyssey: Pepsi to Apple* (New York: Harper & Row: 1987), 6–7.

28. Ibid., 6.

29. R. Simons and H. Weston, "USA Today," Case 9–191-004 (Boston: Harvard Business School, 1991).

30. R. Simons, "Polysar Limited," Case 9–187-098 (Boston: Harvard Business School, 1987).

31. A. Taylor III, "GM's $11 Billion Turnaround," *Fortune*, October 17, 1994.

32. For a discussion of interactive control systems and subjective performance evaluations, see Simons, *Levers of Control*, 117–119.

33. M. T. Hansen and C. Darwell, "Intuit, Inc.: Transforming an Entrepreneurial Company into a Collaborative Organization," Case 9–403-064 (Boston: Harvard Business School, 2003), 9.

34. Hastings, *The New Organization*, 72.

35. Yukl and Falbe, "Influence Tactics and Objectives."

36. Edmondson, "Managing the Risk of Learning," 257.

37. Mikio Fujitsuka, "Honda Motor Company" (MBA paper, Harvard Business School, December 2003).

38. L. Hawkins Jr., "Reversing 80 Years of History: GM Is Reining in Global Fiefs," *New York Times*, October 6, 2004: A1.

39. Kanter et al., *Innovation*, 79–82.

**Chapter 6**

1. Perrow, *Complex Organizations*, 232.

2. Reported in Ghoshal and Bartlett, "Changing the Role of Top Management," 92.

3. Lawrence Summers, address at Harvard Business School symposium on governance, leadership, and values, May 15, 2003.

4. Mintzberg, *Power in and Around Organizations*, 155.

5. Thompson, *Organizations in Action*, 54.

6. L. Wayne, "The Corridor from Goldman to Washington Is Well Traveled," *New York Times*, December 13, 2002. It should be noted that in 1999 Goldman Sachs became a publicly traded company instead of a partnership. It remains to be seen whether the strong culture rooted in shared responsibilities and long-term client relationships will persist now that the business faces the short-term profit pressures of a public company. See S. Butcher, "The Jury Is Out on Culture Change at Goldman Sachs," *Financial Times*, February 22, 2004.

7. See *Fortune* magazine's annual listing of America's most admired companies, which has been compiled and published each March for the past twenty-three years. In this period, Johnson & Johnson has ranked in the top ten most admired companies twelve times.

8. Sherif, "Superordinate Goals in the Reduction of Intergroup Conflict."

9. Collins and Porras, *Built to Last*, 73–78 and chapter 5; R. Warren, *The Purpose-Driven Life: What on Earth Am I Here For?* (Grand Rapids, MI: Zondervan, 2002); quote from Bartlett and Ghoshal, "Changing the Role of Top Management," 84.

10. Mintzberg, *Power in and Around Organizations*, 278.

11. Brian Lannan, "Commitment to Coffee, Commitment to Mission: Why and How Howard Schultz Built Span of Support at Starbucks" (MBA paper, Harvard Business School, December, 2004).

12. Tajfel, "Social Categorization, Social Identity, and Social Comparison," 63.

13. Polzer, "How Subgroup Interests and Reputations Moderate the Effect of Organizational Identification on Cooperation."

14. O'Reilly and Chatman, "Organizational Commitment and Psychological Attachment."

15. R. M. Kramer, "Cooperation and Organizational Identification."

16. Roland Baroni and Chris Goodwin "Commerce Bank" (MBA paper, Harvard Business School, December 2003), drawing in

part on F. X. Frei, "Commerce Bank," Case 9–603-080 (Boston: Harvard Business School, 2003).

17. Pfeffer and Sutton, *The Knowing-Doing Gap*, 189.

18. C. O'Reilly and J. Pfeffer, "Southwest Airlines: Using Human Resources for Competitive Advantage (A)," Case HR-1A (Stanford, CA: Stanford University Graduate School of Business, undated).

19. Ning Tang, "Hawaii Diabetes Disease Management Program" (MBA paper, Harvard Business School, December 2004).

20. Mayer et al., "An Integrative Model of Organization Trust."

21. Rousseau et al., "Not So Different After All," 395.

22. Kramer, "Cooperation and Organizational Identification," 252.

23. Polzer, "How Subgroup Interests and Reputations Moderate the Effect of Organizational Identification on Cooperation."

24. This technique is discussed and illustrated in Krackhardt and Hanson, "Informal Networks."

25. Alex Thatcher, "ArvinMeritor LVS: Aligning the Four Spans" (MBA paper, Harvard Business School, December 2004).

26. Narayanan and Sarkar, "The Impact of Activity-Based Costing on Managerial Decisions at Insteel Industries."

27. Rodgers, *The IBM Way*, 11. Reported in Kirsten Paust, "The Organizational Design Choices of IBM, Southwest Airlines, and P&G" (individual MBA research study, Harvard Business School, April 2003).

28. T. Simons, "The High Cost of Lost Trust"; W. George, *Authentic Leadership*.

29. See, for example, Goold and Campbell, *Designing Effective Organizations*, 41.

30. Khanna and Palepu, "The Right Way to Restructure Conglomerates in Emerging Markets."

31. Details in this section are from C. O'Reilly and J. Pfeffer, "Southwest Airlines: Using Human Resources for Competitive Advantage (A)," Case HR-1A (Stanford, CA: Stanford University Graduate School of Business, undated).

32. B. O'Brian, "Southwest Airlines Is a Rare Carrier: It Still Makes Money," *Wall Street Journal*, October 26, 1992. Reported in O'Reilly and Pfeffer, "Southwest Airlines: Using Human Resources for Competitive Advantage (A)."

33. Analysis prepared by Andrew Glass, untitled MBA paper (Harvard Business School, November, 2004).

34. Tara Purohit and Alix Wilson, "New Sector Alliance" (MBA paper, Harvard Business School, December 2003).

35. H. Mintzberg, R. Simons, and K. Basu, "Beyond Selfishness."

36. J. Helyar, "The Only Company Wal-Mart Fears," *Fortune*, November 24, 2003: 166.

37. G. Morgenson, "Two Pay Packages, Two Different Galaxies," *New York Times*, 4 April 2004: BU 7.

38. S. London, "IBM's New Chief Executive Is Betting That the Company's Future Lies in the Acquisition of a Consulting . . . ," *Financial Times*, October 10, 2003: 17.

39. P. Sellers. "The Trials of John Mack," *Fortune*, September 1, 2003: 106.

40. Pfeffer and Sutton, *The Knowing-Doing Gap*, 179.

41. A. Taylor, "Getting Ford in Gear," *Fortune*, May 12, 2003: 106.

42. Leavitt, "Why Hierarchies Survive," 102.

## Chapter 7

1. S. M. Davis and P. R. Lawrence, "Problems of Matrix Organizations."

## Chapter 8

1. The X test is intended to be directional and suggestive rather than definitive and exact.

2. This analysis was suggested in Lionel Trichard, "Interactive Networks at GE and J&J" (MBA paper, Harvard Business School, December 2003).

3. For a description of interactive control systems at Johnson & Johnson, see R. Simons, "Codman & Shurtleff: Planning and Control System," Case 187–081 (Boston: Harvard Business School, 1987).

4. Bower, "Building the Velcro Organization."

5. Harvard Business School students Takashi Kimiwada and Masayuki Omoto suggested the relationship between the spans and organizational crises.

6. Miller and Friesen, *Organizations: A Quantum View*, 214, 250, 260.

7. This review is based in part on Kirsten Paust, "The Organizational Design Choices of IBM, Southwest Airlines, and P&G" (individual MBA research study, Harvard Business School, April 2003).

8. P. Carroll, *Big Blues: The Unmaking of IBM* (New York: Crown, 1993), 59.

9. R. Simons and H. Weston, "IBM: Make It Your Business," Case 9-190-137 (Boston: Harvard Business School, 1991).

10. D. Kirkpatrick, "Inside Sam's $100 Billion Growth Machine," *Fortune*, June 14, 2004: 80–98.

11. Hemp and Stewart, "Leading Change When Business Is Good: Interview with IBM's Samuel J. Palmisano."

12. Prokesch, "Unleashing the Power of Learning," 18.

13. Lawrence and Nohria, *Driven: How Human Nature Shapes Our Choices.*

14. A. N. Whitehead, *Process and Reality* (New York: Macmillan, 1929), 515.

# BIBLIOGRAPHY

Applegate, L. M., R. D. Austin, and F. W. McFarlan. *Corporate Information Strategy and Management: Text and Cases.* 6th ed. New York: McGraw-Hill, 2003.

Bartlett, C. A., and S. Ghoshal. "Changing the Role of Top Management: Beyond Strategy to Purpose." *Harvard Business Review* 72 (November–December 1994): 79–88.

Bower, J. L. "Building the Velcro Organization: Creating Value Through Integration and Maintaining Organization-Wide Efficiency." *Ivey Business Journal* 68 (November–December 2003): 1–10.

Bradach, J. L. *Franchise Organizations.* Boston: Harvard Business School Press, 1998.

Brickley, J. A., C. W. Smith Jr., and J. L. Zimmerman. *Designing Organizations to Create Value: From Structure to Strategy.* New York: McGraw-Hill, 2003.

Campbell, D., S. Datar, S. Kulp, and V. G. Narayanan. "Using Non-Financial Measures for Evaluating Business Strategy." Unpublished manuscript, 2004.

Chandler, A. D. Jr. *Strategy and Structure: Chapters in the History of the American Industrial Enterprise.* Boston: The MIT Press, 1962.

Coleman, J. S. *Foundations of Social Theory.* Cambridge, MA: Belknap/Harvard University Press, 1990.

Collins, J., and J. I. Porras. *Built to Last.* New York: HarperBusiness, 1994.

Davis, S. M., and P. R. Lawrence. "Problems of Matrix Organizations." *Harvard Business Review* 56 (May–June 1978): 131–139.

Decker, C. L. *Winning with the P&G 99.* New York: Pocket Books, 1998.

Dent, J. F. "Tensions in the Design of Formal Control Systems: A Field Study in a Computer Company." In *Accounting & Management: Field Study Perspectives*, edited by W. J. Bruns Jr. and R. S. Kaplan. Boston: Harvard Business School Press, 1987.

Eccles, R. G. *The Transfer Pricing Problem: A Theory for Practice*. Lexington, MA: Lexington Books, 1985.

Edmondson, A. C. "Managing the Risk of Learning: Psychological Safety in Work Teams." In *International Handbook of Organizational Teamwork and Cooperative Working*, edited by M. A. West, D. Tjosvold, and K. G. Smith. London: Blackwell, 2003.

Galbraith, J. R. *Organization Design*. Reading, MA: Addison-Wesley, 1977.

Galbraith, J. R., D. Downey, and A. Kates. *Designing Dynamic Organizations*. New York: American Management Association, 2002.

George, W. *Authentic Leadership: Rediscovering the Secrets to Creating Lasting Value*. San Francisco: Jossey-Bass, 2003.

Ghoshal, S., and C. A. Bartlett. "Changing the Role of Top Management: Beyond Structure to Process." *Harvard Business Review* 73 (January–February 1995): 86–96.

Goold, M., and A. Campbell. *Designing Effective Organizations*. San Francisco: Jossey-Bass, 2002.

Greiner, L. "Evolution and Revolution as Organizations Grow." *Harvard Business Review* 76 (May–June 1998): 55–68. Originally published in *Harvard Business Review* 50 (July–August 1972).

Hackman, J. R. *Leading Teams*. Boston: Harvard Business School Press, 2002.

Hastings, C. *The New Organization: The Growing Culture of Organizational Networking*. London: McGraw-Hill, 1993.

Hemp, P., and T.A. Stewart. "Leading Change When Business is Good: Interview with IBM's Samuel J. Palmisano." *Harvard Business Review* 82 (December 2004): 60–70.

Johnson, H. T., and R. S. Kaplan. *Relevance Lost: The Rise and Fall of Management Accounting*. Boston: Harvard Business School Press, 1987.

Kanter, R. M., J. Kao, and F. Wiersema. *Innovation*. New York: HarperCollins, 1997.

Kaplan, R. S., and D. P. Norton. *The Balanced Scorecard*. Boston: Harvard Business School Press, 1996.

———. *The Strategy-Focused Organization*. Boston: Harvard Business School Press, 2001.

Kerr, S. "On the Folly of Rewarding A While Hoping for B." *Academy of Management Journal* 18 (December 1975): 769–783.

Khanna, T., and K. Palepu. "The Right Way to Restructure Conglomerates in Emerging Markets." *Harvard Business Review* 77 (July–August 1999): 125–134.

Krackhardt, D., and J. R. Hanson. "Informal Networks: The Company Behind the Chart." *Harvard Business Review* 71 (July–August 1993): 105–111.

Kramer, R. J. *Organizing for Global Competitiveness: The Business Unit Design.* Report 1110. New York: The Conference Board, 1995.

Kramer, R. M. "Cooperation and Organizational Identification." In *Social Psychology in Organizations,* edited by J. K. Murnigham. Englewood Cliffs, NJ: Prentice-Hall, 1993.

Lawrence, P., and J. Lorsch. *Organization and Environment.* Cambridge, MA: Harvard University Press, 1967.

Lawrence, P., and N. Nohria. *Driven: How Human Nature Shapes Our Choices.* San Francisco: Jossey-Bass, 2002.

Leavitt, H. J. "Why Hierarchies Survive." *Harvard Business Review* 81 (March 2003): 96–102.

Levitt, T. "Creativity Is Not Enough." *Harvard Business Review* 80 (August 2002): 137–144. Originally published in 1963.

Magretta, J. "The Power of Vertical Integration: An Interview with Dell Computer's Michael Dell." *Harvard Business Review* 76 (March–April 1998): 73–84.

Massnick, F. *The Customer Is CEO.* New York: American Management Association, 1997.

Mayer, R. C., J. H. Davis, and F. D. Schoorman. "An Integrative Model of Organization Trust." *Academy of Management Review* 20, no. 3 (1995): 709–734.

Merchant, K. A. *Control in Business Organizations.* Marshfield, MA: Ballinger, 1985.

Milgrom, P., and J. Roberts. *Economics, Organization, and Management.* Englewood Cliffs, NJ: Prentice-Hall, 1992.

Miller, D., and P. H. Friesen. *Organizations: A Quantum View.* Englewood Cliffs, NJ: Prentice-Hall, 1984.

Miller, G. "The Magic Number Seven, Plus or Minus Two: Some Limits in Our Capacity for Processing Information." *The Psychological Review* 63, no. 2 (1956): 81–97.

Mintzberg, H. *The Structuring of Organizations.* Englewood Cliffs, NJ: Prentice-Hall, 1979.

——. *Power in and Around Organizations*. Englewood Cliffs, NJ: Prentice-Hall, 1983.

——. "Five Ps for Strategy." *California Management Review* 30, no. 1 (1987): 11–24.

Mintzberg, H., R. Simons, and K. Basu. "Beyond Selfishness." *Sloan Management Review* 44 (Fall 2002): 67–74.

Narayanan, V. G., and R. Sarkar. "The Impact of Activity-Based Costing on Managerial Decisions at Insteel Industries." *Journal of Economics and Management Strategy* 11, no. 2 (2002): 257–288.

O'Reilly, C. III, and J. Chatman. "Organizational Commitment and Psychological Attachment: The Effects of Compliance, Identification, and Internalization on Prosocial Behavior." *Journal of Applied Psychology* 71, no. 3 (1986): 492–499.

Perrow, C. *Complex Organizations*. 3rd ed. New York: Random House, 1986.

Pfeffer, J., and R. I. Sutton. *The Knowing-Doing Gap: How Smart Companies Turn Knowledge into Action*. Boston: Harvard Business School Press, 2000.

Polzer, J. T. "How Subgroup Interests and Reputations Moderate the Effect of Organizational Identification on Cooperation." *Journal of Management* 30 (2004): 71–96.

Porter, M. E. *Competitive Strategy*. New York: The Free Press, 1980.

——. *Competitive Advantage*. New York: The Free Press, 1985.

Prokesch, S. E. "Unleashing the Power of Learning: An Interview with British Petroleum's John Browne." *Harvard Business Review* 75 (September–October 1997): 147–168.

Rodgers. B. *The IBM Way*. New York: Harper & Row, 1986.

Rousseau, D. M., S. B. Sitkin, R. S. Burt, and C. Camerer. "Not So Different After All: A Cross-Discipline View of Trust." *Academy of Management Review* 23, no. 3 (1998): 393–404.

Sherif, M. "Superordinate Goals in the Reduction of Intergroup Conflict." *The American Journal of Sociology* 63, no. 4 (1958): 349–356.

Sheth, J., B. Mittal, and B. Newman. *Customer Behavior*. Fort Worth, TX: Dryden, 1999.

Shuman, J., J. Twombly, and D. Rottenberg. *Everyone Is a Customer*. Chicago: Dearborn Trade Publishing, 2002.

Simon, H. A. *Administrative Behavior: A Study of Decision-making Processes in Administrative Organizations*. Chicago: Macmillan, 1947.

Simons, R. "Strategic Orientation and Top Management Attention to Control Systems." *Strategic Management Journal* 12, no. 1 (1991): 49–62.

———. *Levers of Control: How Managers Use Innovative Control Systems to Drive Strategic Renewal*. Boston: Harvard Business School Press, 1995.

———. "How Risky Is Your Company?" *Harvard Business Review* 77 (May–June 1999): 85–94.

———. *Performance Measurement & Control Systems for Implementing Strategy*. Upper Saddle River, NJ: Prentice-Hall, 2000.

Simons, R., and A. Dávila. "How High Is Your Return on Management?" *Harvard Business Review* 76 (January–February 1998): 71–80.

Simons, T. "The High Cost of Lost Trust." *Harvard Business Review* 80 (September 2002): 18–19.

Stevenson, H., and J. Jarillo. "A Paradigm of Entrepreneurship: Entrepreneurial Management." *Strategic Management Journal* 11 (Summer Special Issue 1990): 17–27.

Tajfel, H. "Social Categorization, Social Identity, and Social Comparison." In *Differentiation Between Social Groups: Studies in the Social Psychology of Intergroup Relations*, edited by H. Tajfel. London: Academic Press, 1978.

Taylor, F. W. "Principles and Methods of Scientific Management." *Journal of Accountancy* 12 (June 1911): 117–124.

Thompson, J. D. *Organizations in Action*. New York: McGraw-Hill, 1967.

Treacy, M., and F. Wiersema. *The Discipline of Market Leaders*. Reading, MA: Addison-Wesley, 1995.

Vancil, R. F. *Decentralization: Managerial Ambiguity by Design*. New York: Financial Executives Research Foundation, 1979.

Van De Ven, A. H., A. L. Delbecq, and R. Koenig. "Determinants of Coordination Modes Within Organizations." *American Sociological Review* 41 (April 1976): 322–338.

Weber, M. *The Protestant Ethic and the Spirit of Capitalism*. Translated from the German by Talcott Parsons. New York: Scribner, 1930.

Wilson, J. Q. *Bureaucracy: What Government Agencies Do and Why They Do It*. New York: Basic Books, 1989.

Wilson, S. *The Man in the Gray Flannel Suit*. New York: Simon and Schuster, 1955.

Yukl, G., and C. M. Falbe. "Influence Tactics and Objectives in Upward, Downward, and Lateral Influence Attempts." *Journal of Applied Psychology* 75, no. 2 (1990): 132–140.

# Index

# ABOUT THE AUTHOR

*Robert Simons* is the Charles M. Williams Professor of Business Administration at Harvard Business School, where he teaches courses on strategy implementation, management control, and organization design. Simons has served as head of the school's Accounting & Control faculty unit and as director of the division of research. He is currently chairman of the Advanced Management Program for senior executives. Simons's first book, *Levers of Control: How Managers Use Innovative Control Systems to Drive Strategic Renewal* (HBS Press, 1995), won the award for Notable Contribution to Management Accounting Literature.